THE FORMULA OF LIFE

THE FORMULA OF LIFE

GO DEEPER
RISE HIGHER

RENA HARVEY

Copyright © Rena Harvey 2024
First published by the kind press 2024

The moral right of the author to be identified as the author of this work has been asserted.

All rights reserved. Without limiting the rights under copyright reserved above, no part of this publication may be reproduced, stored in or introduced into a retrieval system, or transmitted, in any form or by any means (electronic, mechanical, photocopying, recording or otherwise) without the prior written permission of the publisher of this book.

A catalogue record for this book is available from the National Library of Australia.

Trade Paperback ISBN: 978-1-7635083-0-9
eBook ISBN: 978-1-7635083-1-6

Interior graphics by Jake Drechsel

Print information available on the last page.

We at The Kind Press acknowledge that Aboriginal and Torres Strait Islander peoples are the Traditional Custodians and the first storytellers of the lands on which we live and work; and we pay our respects to Elders past and present.

THE
KIND
PRESS

www.thekindpress.com

We advise that the information contained in this book does not negate personal responsibility on the part of the reader for their own wellbeing, health and safety. The intent of the author is only to offer helpful and informative material on the subjects. While the publisher and author have used their best efforts in preparing this book, the material in this book is of the nature of general comment only. It is sold with the understanding that the author and publisher are not engaged in rendering advice or any other kind of personal or professional service in the book. In the event that you use any of the information in this book for yourself, the author and the publisher assume no responsibility for your actions.

Dedicated to my inner child, to my children and to the future members of my family line.

May this forever empower you.

Love,
Rena Harvey
xx

CONTENTS

Introduction	1
Four Pieces Of The Pie And The Six Powerful Principles	9
Trust Me, Trust Yourself, Trust The Process	27
PRINCIPLE 1 Connection To Source, Connection To You	41
PRINCIPLE 2 Reprogramming Childhood Wounding	65
PRINCIPLE 3 Positive Thinking And Creating Alignment	101
PRINCIPLE 4 The Light And Dark Sides Of Your Being	145
PRINCIPLE 5 Feminine And Masculine Power	167
PRINCIPLE 6 Relationships And Soul Contracts	191
Now What?	209
Dear Parents and Future Parents	219
About the Author	224

INTRODUCTION

With absolute certainty, I assure you that this book is destined to bring you significant life changes. As you embark on this journey, embrace the sense of excitement and pride that fate has guided you to the enchanting magic concealed within these pages. Prepare yourself for an extraordinary journey of self-discovery and transformation as you dive into the empowering world of *The Formula of Life*.

This book is a treasure for you to keep and revisit countless times throughout your life.

Through these teachings, you will encounter six powerful principles that will deepen your self-awareness and understanding. Through exercises in each principle, you'll go deeper and rise higher, unlocking greater personal empowerment. Trust the journey ahead and recognise this book as a universal formula we all experience and need to understand. As you undergo this process, your awareness will expand, and profound activation awaits as you explore the various facets of your being and spiritual essence.

The Formula of Life is about you truly understanding who you are. Uncovering all aspects of yourself, living in this reality. It's the formula that we all go through, understanding your human being and aligning it with your spiritual self, so you can truly live to your highest potential, and fully understand what you have created and in turn what you want to create. There is no separation, this is not about religion, or groups, or different cultures, this is about the ONE race—the human race—and you are part of it, and we all go through the same formula no matter where we come from or what we believe.

You are an individual and you are the collective. It's time we *all* rise together and understand ourselves at such a deep level to rise human consciousness.

Before you delve into the principles, you will undertake an introduction exercise to guide you to look vulnerably at your current state and help you create your desired life. I call it the four pieces of your life: health, relationships, lifestyle, career/purpose. By looking at each of these areas, you can have an honest conversation with yourself and determine a solid path to what you really desire.

The Formula of Life is not just a book, though. It is the luminous path to realising your true self, the beginning of a journey that promises to reshape your existence in ways you've never imagined. It's a road to self-mastery and wisdom, unlocking the doors to your fullest potential and igniting the radiant flames of inner transformation. You will discover the depths of your inner self, revealing the extraordinary power that resides within you—a power to heal, to transform, to love yourself—to receive and create your ultimate life.

Within these pages, you will embark on the very journey I'm describing. You'll learn the potent teachings that have not only guided me, but have also transformed the lives of countless clients, leading them towards a purposeful existence and the attainment of profound healing.

The Formula of Life is your guiding light on a journey to the understanding of self, power and truth. It offers you the tools to unravel the layers of your being, shedding light on those aspects that hinder your path to becoming the best version of yourself. You'll learn how to cultivate a firm foundation for change by up-levelling your thoughts, your feelings and your reality.

However, we've all felt at times like life is a game without a rule book, like we're trapped or lost and victimised by circumstances beyond our control. But to truly win at this game of life, we need to shift our awareness of self, detach from personalising our circumstances and life experiences and discover how to shift our limitations into power and create true freedom and success.

This book is about more than just achieving external success—it's about cultivating a firm foundation for real, lasting change. It's an empowering quest to confront limiting beliefs and unearth the very thoughts that reside in the depths of your subconscious. This exploration will grant you invaluable insights into the programming that has shaped your existence.

If you're tired of feeling trapped, stuck, lacking in clarity and motivation and you are ready to transform your life from one of wounding, trauma and pain into one of health, happiness and power, then *The Formula of Life* is for you. It's easy to fall into believing we're just playing the cards we've been dealt. We try to manage our lives through unhealthy coping mechanisms like addiction or isolation. But here's the truth. We have total control over our lives, and we can move ourselves into any state we desire. Only then can we draw all the pieces together for a deeper understanding of how real change can occur. *The Formula of Life* will guide you through elevating to a new awareness within and provide you with the necessary tools to fulfil all aspects of your life, connect you to the core of your being and embody the best version of yourself. You are living the most intricate, emotional, powerful and beautiful experience one can have as a soul—human life.

You have the opportunity to move from a mere existence to a life that is truly felt and purposefully lived. The journey to your ultimate self begins here. The possibilities that await you are awe-inspiring. It's time to awaken the dormant power within you and manifest a life that radiates with purpose and fulfilment. A journey to liberate your mind from the clutches of negativity, unveiling a deeper understanding of yourself. It is in this process that you'll come to know your truth, as you stand on the threshold of self-realisation and step into a brighter, more authentic version of yourself.

The creation of anything truly powerful follows a meticulous journey. It is both majestic and a natural unfoldment. All that is needed is consistent dedication, commitment and passion. When you encounter a deep resonance within your soul, you will unmistakably know that you are firmly on the path to greatness.

For me, this was *The Formula of Life*.

My heartfelt wish for you is to unleash the boundless power within you, to define your own truth and to live a life of unparalleled greatness. May this transformative journey touch your soul so deeply that it sparks incredible change in your life. May you realise your fullest potential, heal your pain and boldly step into your authentic self. Recognise that you are the most incredible living being on this planet Earth, poised for extraordinary heights. Alongside this, I wish for you to discover your purpose, allowing you to unleash your creativity, serve and inspire humanity to become better.

Remember, it all starts with you. With humility, I offer my wisdom to serve humanity. Now, it has become my sacred mission and privilege to share this transformative knowledge with you. I put what I'd learnt into practice. It was not enough for me to simply understand the formula intellectually. I had to put in the work and apply it to my daily life. I watched in amazement as I transformed my life from a place of wounding, trauma and pain to one of health, happiness and power. My own personal experience is a testament to the effectiveness of this formula. It was a natural progression for me to share this work with others, as I believe it has the power to positively impact people's lives. My firm belief is that anyone who is willing to put in the work and follow this formula can achieve the results they desire.

My life has been an epic quest, an unwavering odyssey to heal my wounds and unearth the profound purpose that lay dormant within me. I embarked on a pursuit of extensive knowledge that enabled me to unravel the intricate web of spiritual and human existence. Over the past thirty years, I obsessively devoted and dedicated my time to healing and studying all aspects of the spiritual world. Through exploring countless paths, I encompassed numerous techniques, courses, workshops, activities, methods and modalities. I yearned to explore my inner self and gain a true understanding of who I am. I desired to delve into the depths of my own existence, and I wanted to find authentic happiness, boundless freedom and inner serenity. Even though I had already acquired a lot of knowledge, I realised the importance of gaining more. Every time I gained insight from various spiritual teachers, professors, psychologists, scientists and gurus, I discovered that each of them had brought forward valuable understandings and processes to help me achieve my desired reality. I found many significant threads, yet I couldn't shake the feeling that something was missing, that the tapestry was not yet complete.

Despite the wealth of information available to me, I came to realise that no single teacher could provide me with all the wisdom I was seeking. One would show me the intricacies of childhood trauma but leave me wondering about the importance of understanding the light and dark parts of myself. The next would teach me how to use my mind to heal my body, however, leave out how to keep my mind positive. Just as I thought I had solved one problem, another challenge would reveal itself. Each teacher seemed to focus on one particular element, leaving me searching for the missing pieces on my journey towards true healing.

My desire was for the entire picture to come into perfect clarity. So, I persisted in my quest to uncover those elusive missing pieces and bring them all into one place known as *The Formula of Life*.

As I delved deeper into this journey, a multitude of layers unveiled themselves. My unwavering mission began to take shape as I meticulously started to peel back each layer, revealing the core of our existence. I began discovering what was really needed to fully overcome limitations and achieve true liberation. I've spent time integrating all the knowledge I have acquired and collating the information that has come my way. As I began, profound realisations began to emerge, discernment of what was truly significant, what proved effective and the reasons behind what didn't. It was during this process that I became aware of the fundamental elements necessary for genuine healing and dramatic transformation to take root. After decades of dedication and commitment, I began to experience real change within myself. I witnessed a remarkable metamorphosis unfolding as I began to grasp the concept that life itself follows a formula, a universal journey that we all undertake. It became clear that as we master each part of this equation, we gain clear insight and are able to achieve truly remarkable results. Each of us on Earth possesses this unique formula. My purpose, driven by unyielding passion, was to master this and thrive within its design.

It was during the three workshops I conducted between 2015 and 2018, initially named *'Empower the I'*, *'Stepping into Your Power'* and later *'Unleash Your Warrior'*, that I began to witness a threading of knowledge unfolding right before me. The transformation of my clients was the proof that it worked. At this point, I started to connect the dots, realising that the principles I had pieced together over time had culminated in what I now call *The Formula of Life.*

I stripped away all the mysticism and woo-woo and went straight for the essence of delivering it in an easy and logical way. Creating a framework would finally allow me and others to achieve a purposeful and fulfilling life by getting straight to the point.

As I began to witness the remarkable results stemming from applying these principles, I decided to introduce them to my clients in my practice. As a healer, I have the privilege of working with clients in one-on-one sessions. I began using the formula that helped me better understand and test my methods. The results were nothing short of profound, not just for me, but for my clients as well. At this juncture, I realised I had finally unearthed the elusive keys to unlock our fullest potential.

Whenever I work with a client, I guide them on their healing path using the knowledge outlined in this book.

See, a healer isn't someone who magically fixes you. Instead, they're someone who creates a safe space for you to tap into your inner healer and take charge of your own healing journey. This book will provide you with all the necessary principles to awaken your own healer, giving you the tools and techniques to empower yourself and step into your power.

FOUR PIECES OF THE PIE AND THE SIX POWERFUL PRINCIPLES

First, you should understand your current situation and where you want to be in life. Before you start making any big changes, it's crucial to be honest with yourself and open about where you stand right now. This step will help you figure out what changes you need to make. This chapter is all about laying the groundwork for your ideal life. And then, by following the six principles outlined in this book, you'll gain the knowledge and tools you need to reach your goals and create the life you want.

Take a moment to reflect on these areas: health, lifestyle, relationships, career/purpose. Are they full of abundance, or do you feel a sense of lack in any of these areas? We often don't realise that our thoughts and emotions create our own reality. If you're experiencing a lack, it's because of subconscious beliefs that limit your possibilities.

This book has been designed to create new awareness and provide you with the tools to fulfil all aspects of your life. It will help you connect with the core of your being, embody the best version of yourself and live authentically and powerfully.

The four pieces of your pie are:

1. HEALTH

Do you feel well? Do you have vitality and energy? Do you have diseases or physical pain? Do you love your body? Do you love your physicality? What is your mental state like?

2. LIFESTYLE

Are you happy with your environment? Are you experiencing your desired lifestyle? Do you have everything you want? Are you financially free? Are you enjoying life? Are you enjoying your hobbies and interests?

3. RELATIONSHIPS

Do you like your own company? Do you value yourself? Are your relationships healthy? Do you communicate your needs? Do you feel supported in your relationships? Where are you harbouring resentment? Are any of your relationships toxic or co-dependent?

4. CAREER AND PURPOSE

Does your work excite you? Does it connect with your purpose? Do you know what your true purpose is? What are you here to express? What are your unique gifts?

I invite you to engage with the following exercise, designed to facilitate a deep understanding of your current life and your desired life in these four crucial areas.

This exercise will empower you to reflect and focus on your journey so far, acknowledge your present circumstances and then set your sights on manifesting the life you truly desire.

Below, you'll find two example pie charts and two empty pie charts.

The first pie represents your current state of life. I urge you to be sincere with yourself as you jot down your current status in each segment of the pie.

The second pie chart represents your desired future state of life. It's where you want to be. Be specific and concentrate on the achievements you aspire to reach. Don't get bogged down by the details. Simply let your imagination roam freely as you envision the future you long to create.

Current State of Life:

Client's Example

Desired State of Life:

Client's Example

Current State of Life:

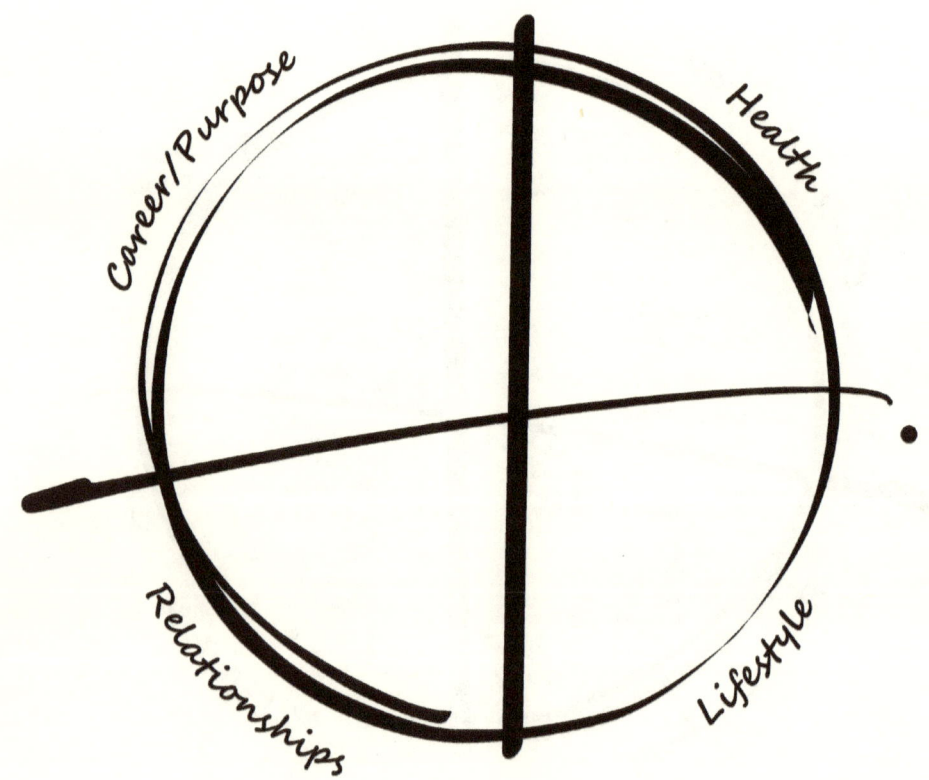

Desired State of Life:

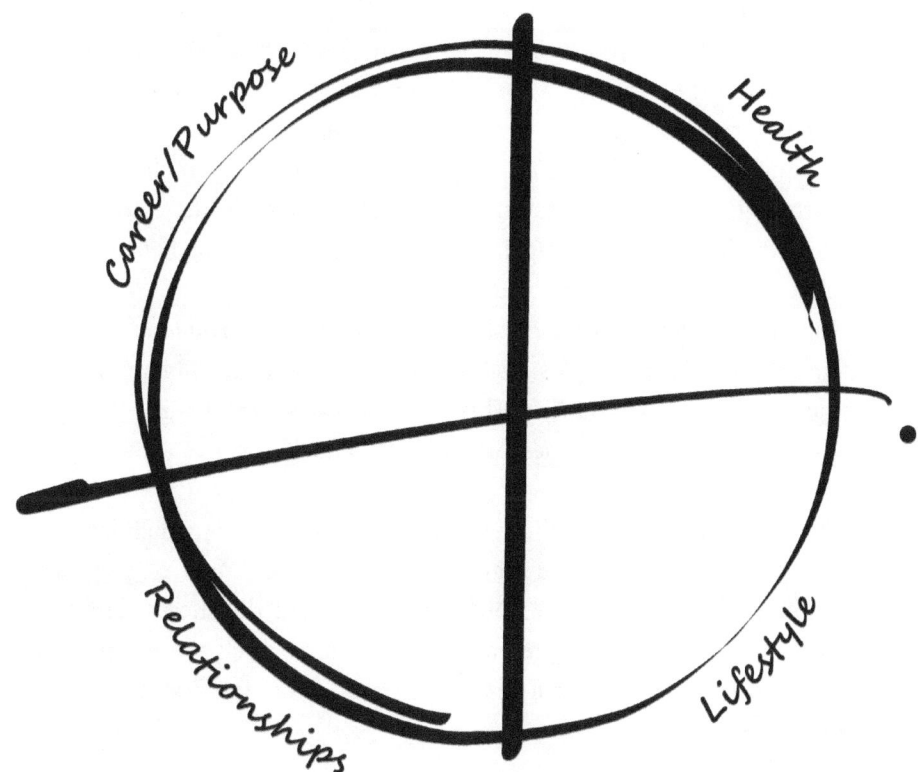

Now that you have identified where you are and where you want to be, you can move on to a more comprehensive understanding of the six principles that will create a firm foundation from which you can make the changes you desire.

How does your current pie look? Is it full and abundant in every slice, or is there a sense of lack and limitation? It's time to up-level each piece and make your pie the best it can be! Having defined your desired life, it's time to immerse yourself fully in the experience of already living it.

No longer should you dwell on your current state of life, because from this point onward, it belongs to the past. Every day from this moment forwards, allow the thoughts and feelings of your desired life to inundate your being, as if it's already yours. As you channel your thoughts and feelings towards your desired state of life, you are starting the journey to making it your reality, closing the gap between what you have now and what you want.

To enhance and elevate each slice of your pie, *The Formula of Life* offers six powerful principles that, when fully embraced, will have an immediate impact on your life. This formula is a powerful guide that will help you embody the best version of yourself and live a life of abundance and success.

By taking action, understanding and implementing these principles, you will witness a profound transformation in every area of your life. You'll be amazed at how quickly you'll achieve the success and fulfilment you've always wanted and understand yourself at a deeper level. It's time to take control of your life and create the reality you truly desire.

The Six Principles of *The Formula of Life* are:
1. Connection to Source, Connection to You
2. Reprogramming Childhood Wounding
3. Positive Thinking and Creating Alignment
4. The Light and Dark Sides of Your Being
5. Feminine and Masculine Power
6. Relationships and Soul Contracts

If you have ever asked yourself any of these questions ...
- Why am I yet to accept and love myself fully?
- Why am I still repeating the same lessons?
- How do I balance my masculine and feminine power?
- Why am I struggling to make ends meet?
- Why does my life always feel like a rollercoaster ride?
- Why am I attracting the same types of people in my life?
- Why am I getting charged up and triggered by others?
- Why aren't things working out for me?
- Why can't I let go and feel stuck in the past?
- Why am I always struggling?
- Is this it? Should I just accept my life as it is?

... Then it's time to implement the principles of *The Formula of Life*.

Clarity forms the foundation of power, as becoming more conscious and aware of your reality is essential. Without clarity, you may find yourself repeating the same lessons and struggling to move forwards. It requires a willingness to continuously learn, grow and evolve. With dedication and a commitment to personal growth, you can unlock your full potential. It's all about understanding yourself at a deeper level and embracing both your assertive, action-oriented side and your intuitive, receptive side. By doing so, you create a harmonious balance that allows you to move forwards with great ease and flow.

Another important aspect of clarity is learning to accept and love yourself fully. This means letting go of self-doubt, negative self-talk and embracing your strengths and weaknesses with compassion and understanding. By doing so, you can release the past and move forwards with confidence and purpose. This means seeking out resources and tools that can help you expand your understanding of yourself and the world around you. By expanding your knowledge and gaining new insights, you can elevate your consciousness and create a reality that is more aligned with your goals and values.

By embracing clarity, self-empowerment and wisdom, you can overcome the challenges that are holding you back and create a reality that is truly aligned with your highest self. If you're asking yourself any of the questions listed before, know that you have the power within you to create the life you truly desire.

Within the pages of this book, you will learn six foundational principles, clearly structured into individual chapters. Each chapter will provide you with a comprehensive exploration of these principles, accompanied by purposeful activities and exercises meticulously designed to foster a deeper comprehension and application of the concepts presented. These easy and practical learnings will give you the opportunity to gain a heightened understanding, to go deeper all in order to rise higher. By actively engaging with the activities and exercises, you will acquire the tools necessary to not only grasp the principles in their entirety but also effectively apply them, thereby maximising your potential for personal growth and transformation.

Let's have a close look at what you will gain clarity on.

1. CONNECTION TO SOURCE, CONNECTION TO YOU

This is about exploring the profound sense of connection to your inner self and the universe that surrounds you. By understanding that source is consciousness and that you are an intricate part of it, you can tap into your highest potential.

Learning to connect to your inner source and the universe around you is a transformative process that can help you develop a sense of peace, purpose and fulfilment. Connecting with your spiritual being and knowing you are a human being having this 'life experience' is integral to your healing journey.

Energy is an essential component of this connection. By understanding its flow, frequency and vibration, you can learn to channel it in ways that can help you achieve your goals and transform your life. This understanding empowers you to create a positive, loving relationship with yourself and the world around you, and enables you to find the balance and harmony you seek.

Lastly, you will unveil the separate channels of your being and how to balance them so they can work in unison. This will guide you to pure consciousness and discovering your purpose.

2. REPROGRAMMING CHILDHOOD WOUNDING

This refers to the process of recognising and transforming negative beliefs and patterns that were imprinted in your psyche during the formative years up to the age of ten. These beliefs and patterns can create limitations and hinder your personal growth because the inner (wounded) child within you is constantly seeking evidence to confirm the truth of these beliefs throughout your life.

Through this process, you will discover how to reprogram these negative subconscious beliefs and break free to reclaim your power and self-worth. By doing so, you can gain a greater sense of control over your life and release the negative impact of past experiences.

This process involves delving deep into your subconscious mind and bringing awareness to the beliefs and patterns that were formed during childhood. By identifying and reprogramming these negative beliefs, you can begin to create new, empowering beliefs that support your personal growth and wellbeing.

This can be a challenging but transformative process that can lead to greater self-awareness and personal fulfilment. Ultimately, reprogramming childhood wounding is about taking responsibility for your own healing and growth. By acknowledging and transforming negative beliefs and patterns, you can create a more positive life for yourself.

You will recognise that these patterns and beliefs have been holding you back and use your newfound knowledge to guide you to live a more confident and authentic life.

3. POSITIVE THINKING AND CREATING ALIGNMENT

To create the life you desire, it is essential to intentionally focus on positive thoughts and emotions to align your actions and choices with your goals and values. First and foremost, you need to identify the thoughts you have, particularly those of a negative nature, and then work on transforming them into new positive ones.

This principle will teach you how to cultivate a more positive outlook on life and bring about your desired outcomes. To understand this process better, it is important to learn about the concepts of vibration and frequency and the laws of the universe that govern them. By doing so, you can learn to manipulate energy for your ultimate achievements. The universe operates on the principles of energy, vibration and frequency. Everything in the universe, including humans, is made up of energy that influences our being.

Each person has a unique vibration and frequency, which can be influenced by their thoughts, emotions and actions. By intentionally focusing on positive thoughts and emotions, you can raise your vibration and attract positive energy into your life. This positive energy can then be harnessed to create the life you desire, with you ultimately becoming a master manifestor.

4. THE LIGHT AND DARK SIDES OF YOUR BEING

In this principle, you will learn about the light and dark sides of your being and the importance of embracing all aspects of yourself. This involves finding a balance between the two, as both are necessary for growth and wholeness. By acknowledging and embracing your shadow side, you can gain a deeper understanding of yourself and your experiences.

By embracing both aspects of yourself in equal measure, you pave the path towards wholeness and self-integration. Understanding the inherent strengths and limitations of these contrasting elements is essential to navigating your journey towards personal evolution. By integrating both the light and dark aspects of your being, you create a state of internal equilibrium. This holistic approach acknowledges the multifaceted nature of the human experience, promoting self-acceptance and nurturing a sense of completeness within oneself. Through this process, you will cultivate a heightened understanding of your own complexities, leading to greater self-love and compassion. You will discover where these dualities serve you and serve others, whilst also highlighting where they don't serve you and don't serve others. The results are mind-blowing. Trust me, you will be shocked at your findings.

It's important to recognise that each side serves a purpose and can provide valuable lessons. By loving and accepting both sides, you can become a more integrated person. Ultimately, embracing both your light and dark sides can lead to greater self-awareness, inner peace and personal growth, making you whole. Both the luminous and shadowed aspects will help you uncover the deep truth that every facet of your being is valuable. Both your light and darkness are essential for a life that is wholesome and in harmony.

5. FEMININE AND MASCULINE POWER

Here you will learn more about the relationship with yourself and the importance of embracing and uniting both your feminine and masculine power, knowing and realising that the relationship with yourself is the greatest love you will ever experience. This means recognising and balancing your assertive, action-oriented side with your intuitive, creative and receptive side. By doing so, you can achieve a harmonious balance that allows you to move forwards in life with greater ease and flow.

When both your feminine and masculine sides are united, you will be in balance with yourself and this will be reflected in your relationships with others, both in your intimate and platonic relationships. In this principle, you will learn about the unique strengths and qualities of both the feminine and masculine energy and how they can work together to bring about positive change in your life. By recognising and nurturing these energies within yourself, you can become a more empowered and balanced individual. In the grand scheme of things, the relationship you have with yourself stands as the paramount connection. It serves as a catalyst, shaping the quality of all other relationships in your life.

6. RELATIONSHIPS AND SOUL CONTRACTS

Finally, you will understand the role that others play in your life and the lessons they are here to teach you. Discovering the soul contracts you signed up for allows you to embrace these lessons.

In our journey of personal growth and awareness, relationships and soul contracts play a crucial role. These contracts are formed and negotiated before we even arrive on Earth. They are our biggest teachers. They are the soul members in our cluster. Each relationship is an opportunity for us to learn valuable lessons and evolve on a soul level.

By understanding the role that others play in our lives, we can begin to see the lessons that are meant to be learnt from each relationship. This helps us to heal our trauma, personally and ancestrally, and cultivate awareness to gain the clarity that helps us on our mission. Ultimately, the lessons we learn through our relationships and soul contracts are designed to set us free. By embracing these lessons, we are free to move forwards on our path of personal evolution with confidence.

Overall, these relationships are here to transform your pain into your power by helping you gain clarity and awareness, cultivate resilience, set boundaries and tap into your own inner strength and wisdom. All this raises you higher into your vibration as a conscious being.

It is vital to understand the importance of learning about all the six principles mentioned because *knowledge is power*. By intentionally connecting to source and yourself, reprogramming your childhood wounding, focusing on positive thoughts and creating alignment, embracing all aspects of your light and dark, balancing your feminine and masculine power and understanding the importance of your relationships and soul contracts, you will reach a divine understanding of your inner self, thus leading you to your elevated consciousness.

I want to remind you of the power that lies within you. You have an immensely powerful ability to transform your *pain into your power*, to create the life you desire and to become the best version of yourself. The principles laid out in *The Formula of Life* have been designed to help you achieve just that. By gaining clarity and knowledge and by tapping into your own inner strength and wisdom, you can create a more positive outlook on life and improve the relationship with yourself and others. As you consistently apply these principles in your daily life, you will embark on a journey of deep introspection and transformation, leading you to new heights of success and fulfilment.

I believe that this *Formula* can be particularly helpful for parents and aspiring parents. The programming years up to age ten are crucial for correcting any emotional wounds and turning them into strengths. By immersing yourself in this book, you can not only improve your own life but also positively impact the lives of your children or future children.

The process of healing is an intricate one, encompassing not only the wounds and traumas of our own lives but also those inherited from our ancestors. It is an essential responsibility to recognise that which remains unresolved within our own ancestral lineage and take proactive steps to address and heal these aspects within ourselves. Failing to address these inherited wounds has profound consequences, as they can manifest as patterns of dysfunction, pain, trauma and emotional distress within our own lives. By choosing to confront and heal these deep-seated wounds, we not only liberate ourselves from their lingering effects, but also safeguard the wellbeing of our children by not burdening them with unresolved ancestral traumas.

By embarking on the transformative journey of personal healing, we pave the way for a healthier, more harmonious future for ourselves and generations to come. Through our conscious efforts to heal, we break free from the patterns of the past, forging a new legacy of resilience, self-awareness and emotional wellbeing. By taking responsibility for our own healing, we empower ourselves and future generations to embrace lives filled with love, compassion and genuine fulfilment.

I invite you to embrace these principles, to go deeper within yourself and to rise higher than you ever thought possible. Remember, you are capable of achieving greatness, and the power to do so lies within you. Let's journey to unlock your greatness together.

Through wholehearted engagement with the principles expounded in this book and their consistent application in your daily life, a profound voyage of introspection and personal transformation awaits you. This journey of self-discovery is bound to propel you towards unprecedented levels of success and genuine healing. As you immerse yourself in these principles, you will ascend to greater heights of personal growth and achievement. The underlying philosophy of *Go Deeper and Rise Higher* encapsulates the essence of this transformative process, urging you to explore the innermost recesses of your being, unlocking hidden potential and ultimately transcending self-imposed limitations. By embracing this path of self-discovery and growth, you will undoubtedly unearth a wealth of untapped resources, allowing you to soar to new horizons of personal and professional excellence.

TRUST ME, TRUST YOURSELF, TRUST THE PROCESS

I am honoured to be the messenger bringing these life-changing teachings and I am here to help pave the way for you to access the depths of your vast potential. So, trust me, trust yourself, trust the process.

The Formula of Life is not just a program. It is a transformational journey that allows you to access your emotional state, uncover your thoughts and beliefs about life and equip you with the tools and techniques needed to succeed in this game. Through this process, you will journey to a place of deep understanding, where you will learn to trust yourself and the process of life and expand beyond any limitations you may have previously experienced.

With *The Formula of Life*, you will unlock the keys to your own freedom, facing challenges head-on and discovering the answers that lie within you. As you gain clarity and make more conscious choices, you will begin to create a life that is truly fulfilling and aligned with your deepest desires. You will gain self-acceptance and a newfound love and trust in yourself, allowing you to navigate confidently through life with ease and grace. This game of life is the ultimate adventure that all eight billion of us humans have committed to experiencing. We are all players, navigating the ups and downs and the twists and turns in this body that assists in our soul's evolution. On a soul level, we have chosen the souls who will accompany us on this journey. Thus, I realised everything was chosen, negotiated and contracted.

I was raised in a tumultuous household, full of drama, abuse and heavy trauma. My daily suffering felt inescapable, which burdened me with anxiety and constant pain. I endured all forms of abuse—mental, physical, psychological, verbal, sexual—within the walls that were supposed to be my safe place. My only escape was my vivid imagination. I would converse with the posters on my walls, a practice I later realised was my human-self connecting to Source and my higher-self. At times, it seemed like the darkness would consume me, but there was a force that kept pulling me through. I learnt through my teachings I had contracted this choice for a reason; the desire to acquire the lessons and experiences necessary to become a compassionate and intuitive healer later in life. I recognised that if I hadn't gone through and emerged from these challenges, how could I guide others in healing their own pain? I realised that this force was preparing me to become a light worker and a healer. It is said that light workers face immense challenges and often navigate through deep traumas and painful life lessons. It's like walking through a dark tunnel, feeling our way through until we emerge into the light and return to love, which is our true nature.

I have always been curious about spiritual growth and fulfilment. Being highly intuitive and sensitive to energy has meant my journey has had both chaotic and peaceful periods and I've learnt to navigate through them with grace and resilience. Through my experiences, I've learnt the importance of quickening my learning process, as sustaining disharmony for long periods of time was not an option.

Through my younger years, every day felt like a journey through darkness that heavily programmed me with limiting beliefs about myself and sent my nervous system spiralling into stress. I finally ventured out on my own at eighteen, where I continued to grapple with the lingering residue of this darkness. My being was afflicted with anger, frustration, irritation, anxiety and an immense lack of self-love. I had become a master at concealing my feelings. I projected an image of being perfectly fine to everyone I encountered, but in actual fact no one could fathom the internal pain that was silently consuming me. It gradually dawned on me that the responsibility for my feelings rested solely with me because, in the end, I was the one who had to bear them. I came to understand that no one really cared because everyone is dealing with their own thoughts, emotions and concerns.

It became clear I had a choice: I could persist in feeling this way and suffering, or I could seek a path to healing and wellbeing. My yearning for happiness and inner peace had transformed into an intense, burning desire like never before. On reflection, it was in my early twenties that my healing journey really commenced, marked by a torrent of emotions, confronting deep-seated triggers and unearthing dormant traumas. I was running away, and all I knew I wanted was to release these burdens and craft a new life illuminated by happiness. In 1999, I bought a one-way ticket to Bangkok and for three years, I backpacked through seventeen countries, searching for myself and personal freedom. I was trying to find meaning to this thing called 'life'.

I wanted to find the happiness I had never felt as a child. All the painful memories of my childhood and adolescence propelled me forwards, which resulted in the beginning of my healing. It was a long and uncomfortable journey to find solace and recovery. No matter how many countries I visited or how many cultures I experienced, the chaos in my mind followed me wherever I went, my own inner demons unshakeable. It was like a giant iceberg I couldn't avoid. Then I realised that the iceberg was my own frozen emotions that I had to thaw and heal.

My travels exposed me to new experiences and people, each of whom helped me discover more about myself. I learnt that the destination wasn't as important as the journey itself. My liberation and healing were ongoing. I tried to embrace the process with dedication and patience. I began to learn that every experience I encountered was part of a greater plan. This plan was contracted on a soul level before I even entered this physical realm. This plan involved certain people and situations, each one playing a vital role in my personal evolution. My journey towards acquiring knowledge was a gradual and solitary process. I didn't have a single mentor to show me the way, so I had to explore various methods on my own. My quest was to understand why I had endured this darkness in my early years and, most importantly, how to liberate myself from it.

Many a time I lost my way, falling back into my old negative beliefs. My mind was overwhelmed by my limiting thoughts, making it painfully clear just how much inner turmoil I was experiencing. At times, it led me down a road of self-destruction. Engulfed in a tumultuous whirlwind of experimentation with drugs, promiscuity and surrounding myself with toxic influences, I often found myself spiralling into an abyss of despair. I had to confront the significant lack of trust and self-respect that had led me to believe I was worthless, and the recurring realisation that I didn't believe I deserved happiness or abundance. Once I understood this, a yearning began to burn within me, urging me on a quest for exploration, healing, travel and the elusive tranquillity that could only be found within. I travelled the world, soaking up spiritual practices from various cultures and began to meditate and journal my thoughts and feelings. I knew I was ready to take my understanding to the next level.

For the next decade, I threw myself into learning from great teachers, gurus, philosophers and spiritual masters. I devoured books, attended workshops and enrolled in courses. The more I learnt, the more I realised that my spiritual journey wasn't just about intellectualising concepts, but about practical application. I began to work on reprogramming my limiting beliefs and turning them into unlimited possibilities. This began the healing of my childhood trauma. It was hard work, but the transformation was worth it. The fire within me burned brighter than ever and I knew that I was on the right path towards my purpose. As I plunged deeper into my spiritual journey, I invested so much in myself. I was determined to have an embodied experience of spiritual principles and make a real shift in my consciousness. I poured my heart, soul and finances into various practices and modalities. From psychosomatic therapy to meditation retreats, from life coaching to tantric workshops, from clairvoyants to mediums, from reiki sessions to shamanic healings, from silent retreats to release ceremonies, from sound healing to deep-release trauma work with psychologists, I did it all.

It was an obsession. It all made me feel alive, inspired and most importantly, helped with my pain as I reconnected to my higher self. I was hungry for knowledge and eager to apply it to my life. It took commitment, motivation, repetition and most of all, discipline. Slowly but surely, I began to know my authentic self and I witnessed my life transform. It was a journey that required perseverance and trust in myself. I learnt to catch my negative thoughts and feelings and flip them into positive ones. I began to be aware of what I was thinking and feeling and brought awareness into my being.

At twenty-four years old, I met my twin flame. I married at twenty-five and embraced motherhood with my first of three children at twenty-six. It was in the presence of my husband that my reflections and life lessons continued to manifest, all with the purpose of aiding my healing journey. Throughout these years, I experienced life's challenges, often feeling like I took one step forward only to be pushed two steps back. I wrestled with a multitude of emotions and at times, tried to avoid my problems when they became overwhelming. Yet these unresolved issues shadowed me persistently because they demanded resolution. At last, I made the conscious decision to confront them head-on, to finally release them, allowing me to move forwards towards a life of peace and freedom.

While it might all sound great on paper, in reality, it felt like I was climbing a steep mountain with loose rubble constantly tumbling into my face. However, I held firm trust in myself and in the Universe, believing wholeheartedly that I would eventually reach the heights of inner peace and freedom. I was willing to go to great lengths to reach those elevated summits. I assure you that if you commit to the journey and put in the effort, you will indeed reap the rewards.

I've spent the last thirty years learning how to understand my power, years of continuous dedication, constant learning and persistent application. I've learnt how to put these lessons into practice to truly understand the deep-seated trauma within me and to truly gain results. This is my gift to you because I wish someone had handed me a book that provided clear guidance on what steps to take, what specific areas to focus on and how to rid myself of the pain within my being. Through my dedicated studies in spiritual growth and healing, I've discovered that the six principles outlined in this book are precisely the guide you need for your healing and complete transformation, ultimately leading you to become the best version of yourself.

So, trust in me, for I've walked this journey and it has led to my success. Trust yourself, for you have the capability on this transformative path. And trust in the process, which has been meticulously tested to equip you with the most effective tools and techniques for your success. *The Formula of Life* will help you overcome limiting beliefs, help heal from trauma and guide you towards inner peace. I'm giving you the essential tools, a step-by-step guide and the crucial principles needed to lead your most fulfilling life.

My mission is to *empower*—to help others find their way and live in their full potential. By sharing these principles, I will guide you along your own path of discovery. It is my wish that, through sharing this understanding, you will also come to see the beauty and purpose behind your own life experiences. You will begin to embrace the notion that everything happens for a reason and that every experience, both positive and negative, is part of your soul's journey towards expansion. If you're reading this, it's because there's something within you that's seeking change, seeking happiness and freedom. That's why we're all here, to evolve and ascend towards our true purpose. As I've come to understand, self-realisation is the ultimate goal of our life's journey, a state of higher consciousness where we are in tune with our ultimate potential. Each step we take towards this realisation allows us to gain wisdom and ascend to higher states of consciousness.

Self-realisation is the moment when we achieve our highest potential and reach a state of unconditional love, where our hearts remain open and receptive to all the goodness life has to offer. It is the ultimate fulfilment of our soul's purpose and the key to unlocking our true identity. By cultivating clarity and awareness of our true selves, we can move beyond our limitations and step into our full potential. And once we do, we can experience a life of freedom and joy that we never thought was possible.

I remember the moments of doubt, the times when I questioned if I was on the right path. But in those moments, I knew I had a purpose, and it was my passion and curiosity that kept me going. The journey wasn't easy, but it was worth it. Now, I can see how each struggle, each setback, was a necessary step in my growth and evolution. It was all part of becoming the person I am today. And I know that the journey isn't over yet. Yes, like everybody, I still have occasional setbacks, but with these principles I manage to recover and return to peace quicker than ever before. There will be more challenges, more struggles, but I am ready for them. I am ready to keep climbing, keep growing and keep learning. It is a process, and luck has nothing to do with it. It is about determination, grit and realising that I am connected to something greater than myself. I know that anyone can discover and live their purpose, as long as they have the same fire in their heart and a drive to succeed. It took lots of trial and error, but most of all it required consistency, dedication and listening to my inner intuition.

Today, I am living out my mission. I am helping and guiding others to find theirs, too. It is a journey filled with joy, gratification and purpose. And I wouldn't have it any other way. As I continue on my healing journey, I realise it's not just about me. It is about something bigger. It is about being a catalyst for change in this world, and about inspiring and empowering others to heal and find their own purpose. I knew that by healing myself, I was not only freeing myself from my own pain but also breaking the cycle of pain and trauma that had been passed down through generations in my family, therefore breaking it for my children and freeing future generations to come.

I've always had a burning desire to find answers to life's perplexing questions. Curiosity and a thirst for solutions have driven me to seek a happy life. It was within this ongoing task that I unearthed so many gems of wisdom, enabling me to craft this extraordinary work ready to be shared with you. I never imagined that my journey would lead me to where I am today. It has been an incredible ride, filled with ups and downs, but every step was leading me to my purpose.

Today, I am a passionate healer and teacher, certified as a Reiki master, a sound therapist and holistic counsellor, sharing my knowledge and gifts with my clients, watching amazing transformations in their lives. Alongside my private practice, I run sound bath meditations and various offerings. Through these practices, I threaded the material together and discovered *The Formula of Life*. It slowly unfolded in front of me, showing me all the necessary concepts I had learnt through the years. I came to realise that this was the formula we all go through in life, and I knew I had channelled the answers we all seek, the keys to unlocking our true potential and empowering ourselves to our greatness.

I explain to my clients that the healing journey resembles a long, dark tunnel. Once you step inside this tunnel of healing, the door behind you firmly shuts, leaving you with no option but to proceed. In the beginning, you're confronted with discomfort, like being slapped across the face over and over again, and because the doors shut behind you, your only option is to continue walking. As you progress, the discomfort gradually lessens, transforming into gentle nudges, still encouraging you to keep moving forwards. Eventually, these nudges evolve into affirming pats on the back. When you make the deliberate choice to enter that tunnel, you are fully aware there is no turning back. The only path is to forge ahead towards the radiant light at the tunnel's end. When you reach that light, you are living in your truth. Understanding yourself completely and finally in control of your thoughts, feelings and reality.

Looking back on my journey, I am filled with gratitude. I never imagined that my obsession with spiritual growth and my desire to help others would lead me to such a fulfilling and rewarding purpose. I have found my calling and there is nothing more satisfying than knowing that I am making a positive impact and serving others. Each page of this book is infused with the Universal Life Force, activating and guiding you towards the knowledge and insights you need to live in your truth and create the life of your dreams. It's like playing a computer game—as you master each level, you upgrade to the next, unlocking new abilities and opportunities along the way. But remember, the real work is up to you. This book is a tool to help you, but it's up to you to commit to the process and do the work. By making a sincere commitment to yourself, you are creating a safety net of support that will help you achieve the results you desire.

So, trust me, trust yourself, trust the process and let's dive in together, knowing that the Universe is conspiring in your favour to help you live your best life. By choosing to undergo this program, it's apparent that you are ready to make a change in your life. By seeking answers, it's evident you want more for yourself, and this is where trust comes in. Trusting yourself is the first step to achieving your goals and living the life you truly desire.

Begin by repeating the affirmation *'I trust myself'* six times. You are now affirming to yourself that you are ready to trust in your own abilities and to take action towards positive change. Trust is a powerful force that can help you to overcome self-doubt, fear and uncertainty. It's important to remember that trust is not a one-time event, but an ongoing process. It requires commitment and the willingness to face challenges and obstacles along the way. But by trusting yourself, you can tap into your intuition and finally step into your truth.

So, if you're ready to stop feeling stuck, unmotivated and uninspired, and to finally start living the life you imagine for yourself, begin by trusting yourself. Trust yourself to do the work, to commit to change and to succeed. Trust the process and trust that you can choose joy, love and peace. The power is within you, so trust yourself and let the transformation begin.

It all starts with trust. By trusting me, yourself and the process, you are opening the door to a world of possibilities and opportunities. You can break free from the past and begin creating your new and desired reality. It's time to let go of the old and embrace the new. Trusting yourself is the foundation of self-love and empowerment. It's about choosing to be in control of your own life, to living authentically and to creating the life that you truly want. Remember, you have the power within you to make this change and by trusting yourself, you can achieve anything you set your mind to.

Let's begin! So proud of you already.

In the vast expansion of the universe lies the infinite potential within you. You are the universe and within you resides the divine essence.

PRINCIPLE 1

CONNECTION TO SOURCE, CONNECTION TO YOU

You are so much more than you know. The truth is you are a spiritual being having a human experience. There is a vast, untapped potential within you that is waiting to be discovered. Your inherent power is far greater than you can imagine. Once you tap into your power, you will be amazed at what you can achieve. But all too often, we underestimate our abilities and settle for a life that falls short of our true power. You are capable of so much more than you currently believe! What if you could tap into a reservoir of power and energy that lies deep within you, just waiting to be unleashed? Let's go deeper now and rise higher to unlock your greater personal empowerment.

Within you, there is a conscious part that is aware of your human self, while also being connected to the vast universe that surrounds you. As you make your spiritual voyage, you'll discover there is no disconnection between your Inner Child, your Human Self and your Higher Self. It is essential to acknowledge and embrace this truth, for it is through this understanding that you can unlock your full potential and live a life of power and poise. You are capable of achieving greatness and it all starts with the connection to Source and the Source's connection to you.

As you come to understand this truth, you free yourself from the limitations that society and others have imposed on you. You come to realise that you are not just a small, insignificant person in the world, you are a powerful being with the ability to create the life of your dreams. You are one with humanity and the Source that created it all.

In fact, Source is embodied in you and you are Source.

Source is *consciousness*. It is also known by various names, like the Universe, Energy, Spirit, Life Force, Prana or even God. Source is the all-encompassing essence of everything. It's both nothing and everything simultaneously. Think of it as an energy field that flows through all things, the force of life itself. You can imagine Source as an endless, boundless sea of energy that contains everything that has ever existed, currently exists, or will exist. Since everything is a part of Source, it knows everything about itself. And you are intricately connected to Source—Source resides within you. You represent the energy that's intertwined with the entirety, and the entirety is a part of you.

In spiritual terms, a conscious person is someone who is aware of their surroundings and can perceive the world without being clouded by personal biases, desires or preconceptions. They consider various perspectives and gather information to make decisions that encompass a broader perspective.

Living consciously as a spiritual practice involves making choices and decisions that consider not just your interests but also the wellbeing of all living beings and the planet. Consciousness is essentially being aware and responsive to what's happening around you. It means you're awake, alert and actively living your life.

Unconsciousness, on the other hand, is the state of not being awake or aware of your surroundings. This happens when you're asleep. Even though you're physically alive, you're not aware of what's happening around you. Your body is functioning, but your awareness is turned off. In the realm of your mind, there are three aspects of consciousness: conscious, subconscious and unconscious. These relate to how aware you are of yourself, covering your mental, emotional and physical aspects.

THE CONSCIOUS MIND

This is your immediate awareness. It's what you're conscious of in the present moment. For instance, you know you're sitting at your desk having conversations with your work colleagues. However, you're aware of your feelings and emotions, and observing your surroundings at the same time. Consciousness, basically, is the awareness of your external and internal existence.

THE SUBCONSCIOUS MIND

These are the thoughts buried deep without you even noticing them. Think of this as an extensive mental database that contains information you're not aware of every day, but you can access when needed. It's like an archive or a filing cabinet storing your life's accumulated knowledge. It includes memories, emotions, thoughts, experiences, less talked-about ideas and underlying beliefs.

THE UNCONSCIOUS MIND

The ego is also known as the unconscious mind. It is the process of the mind that occurs automatically and is where we store things that aren't readily accessible or brought to the surface consciously. It controls many automatic behaviours such as pain, anxiety and conflict. The unconscious mind is powerful because it consists of all the automatic responses, movements and habits that humans do in their daily life.

We all have the ability to become conscious, but first we need to realise what stage we are at.

> **Unconsciousness or Ego:** You are primarily influenced by the external world, following cultural norms without really understanding why. Life seems to happen without clear awareness.

> **Awakening:** You start to become aware of your actions, though you might not fully comprehend the reasons behind them. Curiosity sparks as you question different perspectives.

> **Self-Discovery and Healing:** You gain a deeper understanding of your actions and actively seek to heal and transform. This phase allows you to focus on your inner world, becoming aware and changing your thoughts, emotions and behaviours.

Living Consciously: You view the world objectively and make conscious choices that benefit not only yourself but also the greater whole.

As you choose to live consciously, you establish a powerful connection with your higher self after exploring new depths within. Realising that you hold the master key to your life, you tap into the boundless energy of the Universe, becoming one with the Source. In this moment, you stand fully prepared to craft your own destiny as a true creator. In essence, the entire spiritual journey can be distilled into a simple phrase: *'You create your own reality.'*

This profound truth holds true no matter how deeply one investigates spiritual practices or expands their knowledge on the subject. Yes, you have the power to manifest and create the life you have always imagined. Whatever you can conceive in your mind and feel in your heart, you can bring into reality. Your mind is a super-powerful tool that has the ability to create anything you desire because you are, in essence, *energy*.

At the core of our existence lies the concept of energy. As physical beings, we are made up of matter, including cells, atoms, molecules and proteins. However, we also embody a spiritual essence characterised by energy. This spiritual aspect is manifested through our energetic auric field, which encompasses seven primary focal points known as chakras. These chakras are believed to emanate subtle energy, facilitating optimal function within our organs, mind, and intellect.

But what exactly is energy? Simply put, energy can be defined as the fundamental force that governs all aspects of the universe, from the tiniest subatomic particles to the largest celestial bodies. It is the driving force behind all processes, movements and changes in the world around us, including those within our own bodies and minds. Understanding the nature and power of energy is the key to unlocking the potential for growth, healing and transformation within ourselves and in the world at large. The ability to sense and read energy is a natural human ability that is often overlooked or dismissed. It is often expressed through our intuition, as we have a sense of whether someone or something has 'good' or 'bad' energy. But how do we know this? Is it something we can measure or quantify?

One way we can understand energy is through the concept of vibration. Everything in the universe vibrates at a certain frequency, including our own bodies and emotions. When we encounter someone or something that has a different vibration from our own, we may feel a sense of discomfort or unease. Conversely, when we encounter someone or something with a similar vibration to our own, we may feel a sense of resonance or connection.

This interpretation of energy comes from a combination of our intuition, our past experiences and our present state of mind and body. It is a holistic understanding that considers both the physical and non-physical aspects of our being. By learning to tune into our intuition and becoming more aware of our own energy and vibrations, we can develop a deeper understanding of ourselves and the world around us.

As a super-powerful being, you hold the key to your own destiny. Your thoughts and feelings are the seeds that sprout into the reality you create and experience. You have the power to transform your life, to break free from old patterns and to transcend limitations. All it takes is the willingness to believe in yourself and the courage to act towards your dreams. Remember that you are the author of your own story. You have the power to write a beautiful and empowering narrative. As you tap into your inner power and consciousness, you become a force to be reckoned with. You radiate confidence, joy and positivity. You attract abundance and success effortlessly. When you connect to yourself and trust in the power of the Universe, you begin to trust in your own ability to manifest your desires. To connect with yourself, you must first understand what you are made up of and then unify all the parts of you. It all begins with your internal aspects.

Our inner child, our human self and our higher self all make up our being.

We may not be aware, but these aspects are always communicating with each other. Our responsibility is to build a relationship with each aspect and become receptive to their messages. When we accept and allow these aspects to speak to us, we open channels of support to meet each other's needs. We become skilled at listening to ourselves and our inner guidance because we have all the answers inside of us.

Each aspect of your being is speaking to you, including your body, and there is always another part of you that can come in to support balance and find harmony. By integrating these aspects of yourself, you can become whole and fully aligned with your true nature. This inner alignment allows you to connect with Source and access the infinite wisdom and guidance that is always available to you. To truly connect with the divine Source within you, you must first become aware of and unify all parts of yourself. Your internal aspects include *your Inner Child, your Human Self* and *your Higher Self.*

All of these aspects play a significant role in our lives, communicating with one another constantly, whether we realise it or not.

The Inner Child within us is a pure source of joy, creativity and innocence. I call this the free child. When healed, it allows us to connect with our soul's gifts and bring more magic and wonder into our lives. However, the inner child has an element called the wounded child that holds the trauma, limited beliefs, victim mentality and ego.

The Human Self is there to protect and discipline us, while also allowing our inner (free) child's creativity to flourish—or it can be driven by the wounded child. It has the ability to listen to the higher self when conscious. When it's unconscious, it will be unaware of the higher self. The healed human self is connected to the needs of the free child and the higher self and, therefore, can navigate the world with confidence and ease. The unhealed human self plays out the needs of the wounded child and cannot hear the messages of their higher self.

Lastly, **the Higher Self** is the all-knowing and awakened aspect of ourselves. The Higher Self represents an elevated state of awareness that encompasses both the physical reality and the energy that underlies it. It's a serene mental state where an individual can observe themselves and the entire existence with an impartial, clear, intuitive and all-encompassing awareness, free from the judgment and subjectivity imposed by the physical world.

The higher self is a complex, multi-dimensional entity with the ability to extend its consciousness or aspects of itself into various realities and dimensions for the purpose of growth, learning and experience. Your core existence is essentially a manifestation of your higher self's essence and energy. This higher self is timeless, boundless, non-material and represents your genuine self, otherwise known as your *True Self*.

Between each incarnation in the physical realm, you originate from your higher self and return to it. Think of your higher self as a larger stream of consciousness within the vast river of Source. In essence, your higher self is a unique current within the greater flow of Source energy, signifying your individuality in the grander cosmic scheme. It's *your soul*. Your soul, at its core, represents life itself and is the force that animates the human body. Everything is composed of energy, and energy doesn't vanish but transforms from one state to another. Your soul is this energy, a life force that can change but never truly disappears.

In the physical world, everything is tangible. Your soul's energy becomes the physical being you recognise as yourself. It serves as a bridge, allowing your spirit or higher self to experience life from a new perspective through you. When you embrace and unify all aspects of yourself, you tap into an incredible power as a conscious creator. You break free from the patterns of the past and gain control over your life. Your focus shifts from the narrow perspective of the ego self to a broader, more expansive awareness of the interconnectedness of all things. You begin to live with a sense of conscious unity, recognising that everything you do has an impact on the world around you.

As we expand our awareness, we move beyond our own personal concerns and start to think about how we can serve others and the greater good. It's no longer just about improving our own lives, but about making a positive impact on the world. By focusing on service to others, we unlock a deeper sense of purpose and fulfilment that can't be found through purely self-centred pursuits. In this state of unity consciousness, we become vessels for divine inspiration and creativity. We tap into a higher intelligence that guides us towards our true purpose and helps us make a positive impact in the world. By living in service to others and the collective consciousness, we become an integral part of the greater whole and experience a profound sense of connection and belonging. It's important to understand that we have unlimited possibilities backed by the unlimited power of creation. This power can help us manifest anything we want, whether it's material possessions, spiritual fulfilment or emotional healing. The universe is vast and abundant and it's here for our taking.

Whatever you desire, you have the power to manifest it. Your optimum wellbeing, health, higher purpose and fulfilment are all available to you. Within the depths of your being lies the potential for greatness—a birthright waiting to be claimed. Once you uncover the truth of who you truly are, a world of infinite possibilities opens up before you. It is through tapping into the power of creation that resides within you that you can become the true master of your own life.

You possess the ability to shape your destiny, to mould your existence according to your deepest desires. The power to create the life you yearn for is within your grasp, awaiting your conscious choice. It is a journey of self-discovery, of unravelling the layers that veil your true essence and embracing the fullness of your authentic self. When you awaken to the realisation that you are a creator, a *co-creator* in fact, in the grand tapestry of life, you unlock a realm of boundless potential. You hold the brush that paints the strokes of your reality, become the architect that designs the blueprint of your experiences. Every thought, every intention, every action becomes a brushstroke on the canvas of your life. This innate power resides within you. However, to gain this self-awareness, inner reflection and a deep connection to your inner wisdom, you have to be aware of your thoughts, your beliefs, your feelings and actions. You begin to create your own reality. You begin to understand that you take charge of your life's direction. You become the author of your own story, the director of your own play. It is a beautiful and liberating transition, one that allows you to live a life that is true to your authentic self. So, dare to dream and dream big! Embrace the power within you and trust in the creative force that flows through your being. With every thought, intention and action aligned with your deepest desires, you step into the realm of limitless possibilities. Welcome your birthright as a creator. Let your life become a masterpiece—a reflection of your truest self. To ignite the fire of your power, you must first embrace the truth of your infinite potential. Believe in your power, believe in your worth and believe in your ability to create the life you truly desire. Break free from the mundane and discover your true purpose in life. You may have been caught up in the hustle and bustle of society, struggling to keep up with the demands of everyday life. But now is the time to take a step back and reflect on your true calling.

If you are here on Earth, it's for one reason: to live out your mission.

If you're thinking, *'But I don't know why I'm here'*, don't worry, because the truth is, you actually do have a purpose. There's a part of you, your higher self, that's always guiding you to figure it out. It knows what your purpose is, but sometimes the doubts and insecurities of your human self get in the way—that negative voice inside you that keeps telling you that you're not unique or important. But that couldn't be further from the truth. You have a special role to play in this world, and your presence is crucial to the cycle of life. Your purpose is about finding that one thing that brings you joy, that makes you lose track of time and that requires minimal effort. It's about fine-tuning that quality and expanding it so you can use your natural gifts to serve others and make a positive impact on the world. So, take a step back and reflect on what makes you unique. What brings you joy? What comes naturally to you? What do others praise you for? It's time to reconnect with your special purpose and live a life that's aligned with your true self. Start by exploring your innate gifts and talents.

What comes naturally to you? What did you enjoy doing as a child? Pay attention to the things you do naturally, without any effort. The things you enjoy that light up your soul are often indicators of what you're meant to do in life. Have you ever stopped to think about what makes you truly unique? What is that one thing that comes so effortlessly that you could do it for hours without even realising it? This is your innate gift, your purpose and it's time to reconnect with it.

Keep in mind, your purpose extends beyond just a career. It's about uncovering that unique role you play in serving humanity. We all possess unique abilities and while someone may share the same purpose, it can manifest quite differently in their career. It's not about comparing yourself to others; rather, it's about staying true to yourself. When you're in alignment with your purpose, everything easily falls into place. Remember, your purpose isn't just about you. It's about how you can use your gifts and passions to serve others and make a positive impact in the world. Don't let fear or self-doubt hold you back. You are capable of achieving great things and making a difference.

Think back to your childhood and remember what brought you the most joy, the thing you loved doing without even thinking about it? Maybe you loved to talk. Maybe you loved helping others. Maybe you were a natural leader. Perhaps you were always the one connecting people or coming up with solutions to problems. I want you to uncover the things you did effortlessly as a child, something that if you asked five people who knew you back then, they'd all agree on. We're not seeking activities you were skilled at, rather, we're exploring that innate gift, something you did naturally that was evident to those around you. We're interested in the things you naturally did that had a positive impact on the people around you. This innate gift holds the clue to what you're truly passionate about and what you're meant to do in this world.

Living a purposeful life requires tapping into our higher selves, which holds the key to our mission and calling. It's about surrendering our limiting beliefs and allowing the infinite wisdom of our higher selves to guide us towards our true purpose. The more we create space for this guidance, the more we receive sudden moments of clarity. Living in our purpose doesn't have to be dependent on divine timing or some predetermined plan. Every moment of our life is leading us towards our mission, even if we aren't aware of it. We do our purpose every day without even realising it. Now it's time to claim it and discover careers that are aligned with exactly those gifts we possess.

When I was a child, what did I do naturally? I loved to talk. My parents called me a chatterbox and, although at times I got in trouble for it, I thrived on engaging with people and sharing stories. Even at school, teachers often urged me to be quiet. However, I loved it. I loved connecting with people. As I grew older, I noticed something interesting. Whenever I spoke, people would often have moments of self-realisation. They would open up to me, sharing intimate details of their lives, even in casual settings like a bar. Initially, I questioned why this was happening, but after countless similar experiences, I realised I possessed a unique ability to make people feel comfortable enough to confide in me. It became clear that this gift of mine was something special, aligning perfectly with who I am.

I felt a deep longing to uncover and live out my purpose like never before. It dawned on me that I needed to fully commit to and trust in the burning passion within me, which was even more powerful than I had realised. I had to let go of self-doubt while learning to trust in divine timing and the Universe. I found great joy in connecting with others, offering advice and engaging in meaningful conversations to uplift them. I found fulfilment in empowering people to reach their highest potential and feel inspired about life. It resonated deeply within me—I had discovered my gift, my purpose 'to empower'.

Over the years, I went through numerous trials and errors to truly live in my purpose. Reflecting on my diverse roles as a high school teacher, scuba diver and photographer, I realise that even in those seemingly unrelated pursuits, I was already fulfilling my purpose by connecting with people on a smaller scale. I even explored a career in acting and entertainment, believing I could empower through those mediums, however the Universe had grander plans in store for me.

Every rejection served as a redirection, guiding me towards my true calling. With each phase and growth in my life, my careers evolved, yet I still felt I hadn't quite reached the pinnacle of my purpose. It was a challenging journey, one that required time and perseverance. Yet, I stayed positive, seeking guidance from the Universe to lead me towards my true purpose. I began exploring different ways I could make a meaningful impact on others' lives and how to use my gift to serve them and make a difference. Embracing my passion for spirituality, I took a leap of faith, overcoming fear to become a healer. My desire to inspire and empower others became my profession, demonstrating the fluidity and beauty of living in alignment with one's purpose. It's not a fixed destination but a journey of self-discovery and growth, unfolding as we tap into our gifts and share them with the world. We are always up-levelling, and our highest potential is forever expanding until the end of our days on Earth.

I often work with clients who are struggling to figure out their purpose and I assist them in their journey to discovery. One client's story stands out as an example. During our sessions, I asked him about his childhood and what came naturally to him. He shared that he grew up in a third-world country and would regularly bring loaves of bread and shoes to his less fortunate friends at school. It became clear that his gift was *to help people in need*. He resonated with that a great deal. Over the course of a few sessions, we delved deeper into his aspirations and explored career options that aligned with his purpose. We discovered so many career options that aligned with his desire to help people less fortunate. He also expressed his love for playing soccer and being outdoors, so I explained to him that he could also align his career path with these passions. His core purpose was to help those less fortunate. By connecting his passions with this purpose, he could create a fulfilling and meaningful path in life.

Activities that bring you joy, such as sports, art, or music, can often be aligned with your purpose. However, it's crucial to understand the core value of your purpose and then explore careers that directly resonate with those values, igniting your passion and creating a meaningful connection to your purpose.

He also expressed concerns about lacking formal qualifications. So, we worked on aligning his vibration with gaining the results he desired. Weeks after dedicating time to believing in himself, the Universe reflected back to him exactly what he desired. He found an opportunity to work as a support care worker for an agency that didn't require tertiary-level credentials. They valued kind-hearted individuals with compassion and a need to help others less fortunate in their circumstances. Now he is fully immersed in his purpose, working in that field full time. He deeply loves his clients and finds his work incredibly rewarding. His presence and care contribute to their happiness and growth during the time they spend together. It's a true testament to the power of aligning our purpose with our actions and the deep fulfilment that comes with it. Each one of us has a unique purpose in this world and it is up to us to discover and fulfil it.

When you neglect your mission, you experience a sense of restlessness and disconnection from yourself, leading to various forms of emotional and physical distress. By being present and open to receiving universal energy, you can connect with your true self and gain the clarity needed to fulfil your purpose. It is essential to remain attuned to your emotional state, trusting that the experiences you encounter are there to guide you towards growth and transformation. Even in moments of uncertainty or confusion, you are always connected to a higher source of guidance and wisdom. By tuning in to this divine intelligence and listening to the signs around you, you can tap into your inner power and access the answers you seek.

Remember that you are here for a reason and your mission is calling out to you. Don't let fear or doubt hold you back from living the life you were meant to live. Be present, trust in yourself and let the Universe guide you towards your ultimate destiny. All you have to do is keep being curious.

Here's an exercise to help you uncover your purpose, which you will state in the centre circle. Around it, aim to fill in as many outer circles as you can with various career possibilities aligned with your purpose and what you are passionate about.

Below, I've provided my own example and the client's example as references. This is just the starting point. I've revisited this exercise countless times over the years. While the outer circles have changed, the inner circle, representing my core purpose, has remained constant. I've explored various paths, confronting doubts along the way. If I encountered limiting beliefs about certain career options, I revisited them until I gained the confidence and belief in myself to pursue them. In my outer circles, there are still goals I haven't reached yet, bigger and more complex career paths that require teams of other individuals. I revisit them as often as I can. I trust in the Universe and divine timing to guide me towards them and connect me with like-minded individuals who support my purpose and share my visions on those creations. I am aware that I am always expanding and reaching more of my highest potential every step of the way.

Dream big and get excited. This is just the beginning, and it will ignite the fire within you. As you progress, you'll begin to believe that you're aligning with your true self and the reason you're here, to fulfil your purpose and lead a fulfilling life. The only thing holding you back is yourself, so let go of your limiting beliefs and embrace all the possibilities available to you.

My Example:

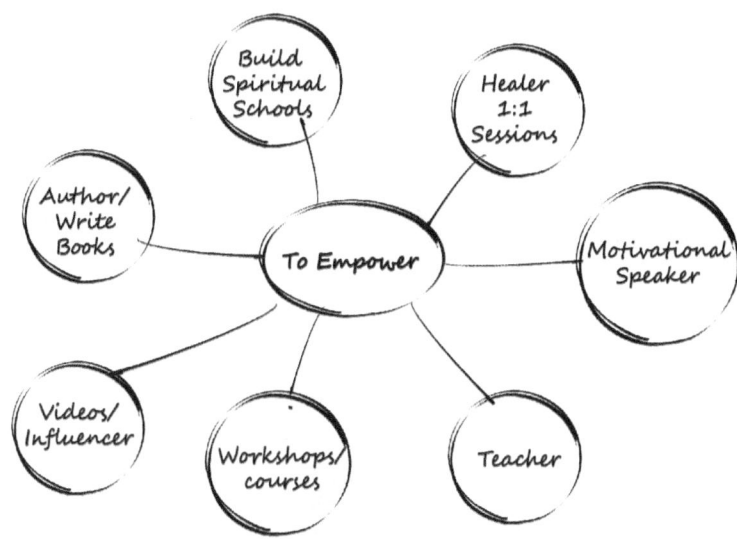

Client's Example:

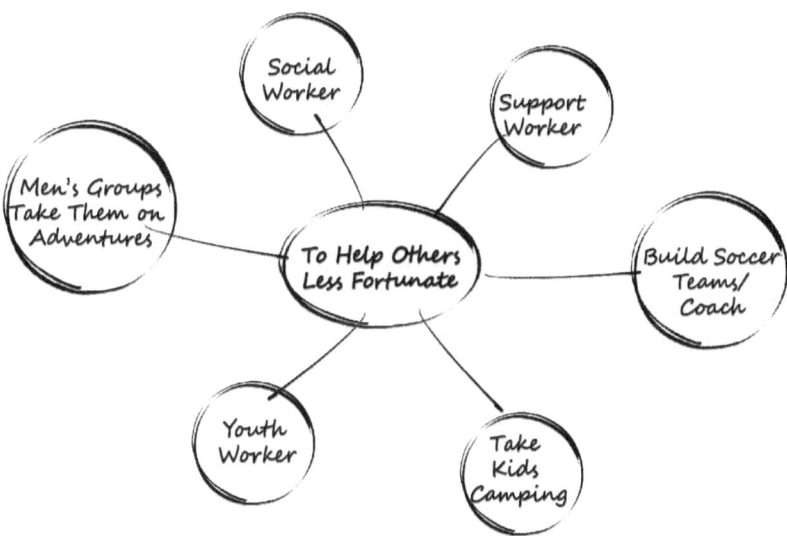

EXERCISE
Discover your purpose

Use this page to reflect back on yourself as a child. Brainstorm using some of the following prompts. If you are struggling, ask family members or people who knew you as a child.

- What came naturally to you?
- What bought you joy?
- What did you do naturally that bought others joy?
- Do you remember some of your favourite things to do? Were they strategy based or individual, and were they indoors or outdoors?
- How did you interact with others? Were you the connector? Were you the class clown? Were you the advisor? Were you the leader?
- What do you still do these days, that you did as a child?

Can you see any patterns? Now form these into one statement to place in the middle of your purpose wheel. Refer to the examples on the previous page if useful, e.g., *'To empower'*, *'To help others less fortunate'*. If you are having trouble, ask five people that knew you as a child. It will all come together, remember it's like a little puzzle unfolding in front of you and you hold the answer. It's not complicated, it's actually quite simple.

E.g. I loved to talk. I inspired people whilst I spoke. I naturally helped them realise things about themselves. I made them feel important and powerful. I empowered them and inspired them. PURPOSE TO EMPOWER!

Your Purpose Wheel:

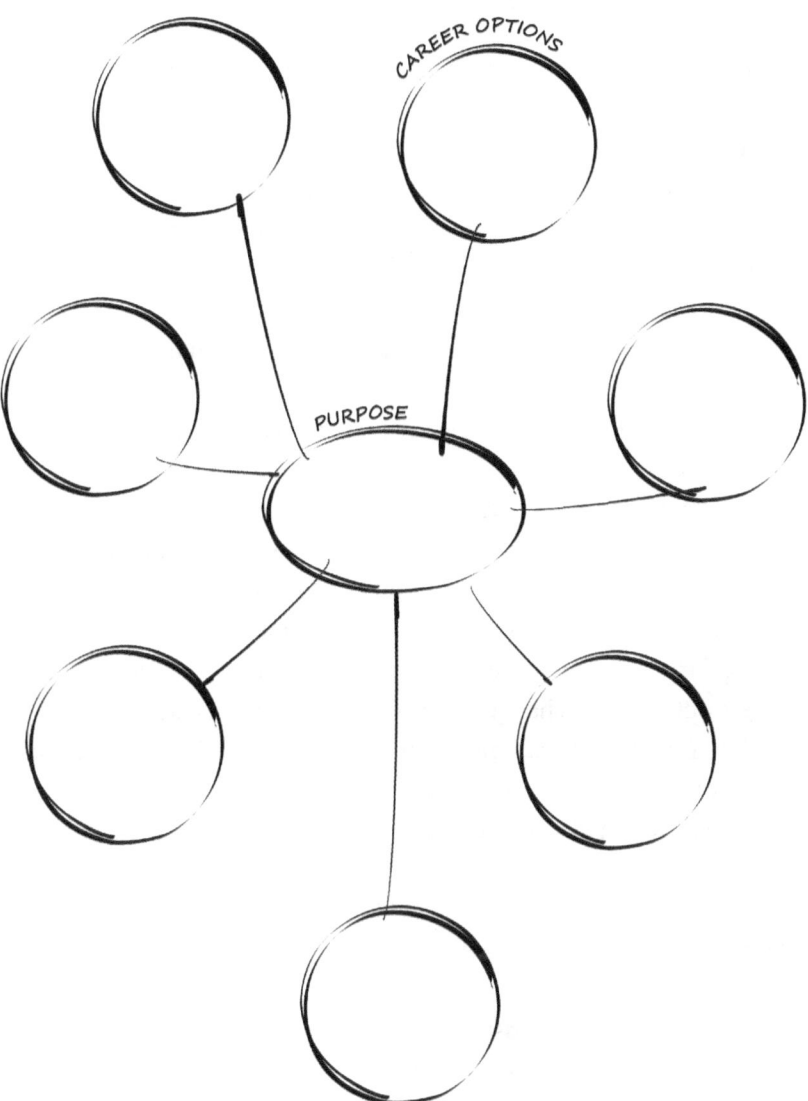

As you engage in this exercise, take note of the career options that resonate with you presently. Are there any that currently align with your life?

Select one and delve deeper. How can you expand upon it? What steps can you take to integrate it into your reality? Consider whether certifications are needed and take the appropriate steps. Start by exploring one career option and allow it to evolve into a fulfilling aspect of your life.

Approach this with confidence, knowing that you are in control of your life. The more you persist and dedicate your energy and focus to one of your career options, the more the Universe will conspire in your favour, aligning you with your true purpose.

This is a journey of expansion that requires both effort and courage to step out of your comfort zone and leave behind jobs that no longer resonate with you.

Now is the time to delve deeper and connect with what you are truly meant to do.

I understand it may feel daunting at times, but don't allow fear to overshadow the exhilaration you'll experience by embracing what comes naturally to you and fulfilling the purpose you're meant for.

Feel free to revisit this exercise as often as you like. This allows you to regularly fine-tune what resonates with you and what doesn't. Some career options may change or be completely replaced as you grow and evolve. Your preferences may shift and what resonates with you today may not in the future. However, by keeping your purpose in mind it will guide you in discerning which options are truly aligned with your higher self.

For now, ask yourself, 'If I could have one of these options in my present reality, which one would have the most positive impact on me and my life?'

This option will most definitely jump out at you. Highlight that career option and make a list of everything you have to do to accomplish it. Take action, set deadlines and dedicate energy towards it for at least ten minutes a day.

Personally, it took me so long after doing this exercise to truly align my purpose with my career options. It wasn't an easy journey—I battled doubts, feelings of unworthiness and insecurities about stepping into my truth. I constantly found excuses, convincing myself I wasn't good enough and comparing myself to others in the field.

However, over that time, I worked on dismantling my limiting beliefs and shedding anything that didn't serve me. During this time, the Universe presented countless opportunities that validated my worthiness and affirmed my birthright to live a life aligned with my purpose.

I rose to the occasion, stepped into my power and now I'm deeply grateful to live in my purpose and do what I love every day. It fills my heart with fulfilment, knowing that I serve others. And I wholeheartedly believe that you can do the same—I believe in you.

Welcome to your purpose!

Within the wounds of the inner child lies the strength to heal, grow and transform into a resilient adult.

INCIPLE

2

REPROGRAMMING CHILDHOOD WOUNDING

I was intrigued by Google's definition of *The Formula of Life*, so I looked it up. It read, *"The secret formula of life, first expressed by Viktor Frankl, an Austrian psychiatrist and Holocaust survivor, can be simplified as follows: Events (E) + Response (R) = Outcome (O)."*

The website was medium.com where experts share their perspectives on various topics. This formula indicates that the outcomes we attain are based on the events that occur, plus the responses we have to them. In essence, it signifies that our success, wellbeing and relationships are contingent upon how we choose to react and engage with the circumstances and situations we encounter. In simpler terms, we are fully responsible for our lives, both the good and the bad. For most people, their formula is simply E (events) = O (outcome). They are merely passengers, with no power to control their direction. By embracing this principle, however, we realise that our triumphs, wellbeing and harmonious relationships depend on how we *choose to respond* to the events we encounter. Our responses play a crucial role in shaping the trajectory of our lives. It's not the events themselves that determine our achievements and happiness, but rather our conscious reactions to them. Internalising this concept empowers us to take control of our destinies and steer our lives towards remarkable outcomes.

For example:
- Some people might say, 'My maths teacher is not good at teaching (Event), so I didn't learn much (Response) and so I failed my maths exams (Outcome).'
- Others might say, 'I don't have the same running shoes as Usain Bolt (Event), so I can't run as fast as he can (Response), therefore I didn't win the race (Outcome).'
- Some might say, 'Obesity runs in my family (Event), so I'll never be able to lose weight (Response), and that's why I will always be fat (Outcome).'

Do you notice a common characteristic among these examples? These individuals tend to blame the events that happen to them and allow them to determine the outcomes of their lives.

Instead, my mission is centred around equipping individuals with the necessary tools to cultivate a transformative approach in responding to life's events. By empowering you to navigate your life with a profound sense of responsibility, my aim is to guide you towards a path of complete fulfilment and purpose.

Let's explore further the vital formula encapsulated by the acronym $E + R = O$. It represents the interplay between events, responses and outcomes, shaping the narrative of our lives. By assigning meaning to the events we encounter, we actively participate in the continuous creation of our own outcomes. Throughout the pages that follow, I will meticulously break down each component of this formula, providing you with a comprehensive understanding of its intricate workings. By the end of this chapter, you will gain a clear comprehension of the concept as a whole, allowing you to harness its transformative power in your own life. It is time to go deeper and rise higher.

You will discover your deep-seated beliefs and uncover any past traumas that may be holding you back. You'll gain insight into the beliefs that limit you and learn how to reprogram them into positive ones. This process will empower you to unlock your full potential and live your best life. Let me explain it to you.

Within the depths of your existence, the seeds of your life's journey are sown, intertwined with the pattern of childhood wounding and programming. It is during these formative years, up to the age of ten, that important events can leave an indelible mark upon your being. In these formative years of childhood, stories unfold (Event), sometimes casting a shadow of negativity upon our young self. We attach meanings to these events/stories (Response), weaving a narrative that becomes interwoven with our very being. Each event carries within it a potent feeling, leaving an imprint upon our subconscious. The meaning (Outcome) we place on these stories becomes the core of our trauma.

Take, for instance, the example of a father departing for work, but in that instance the child is longing for companionship and asking for playtime. The simple response, 'I have to go to work,' even though uttered with good intentions, is received by the child as negative because she didn't get what she wanted. Sadness and a sense of loneliness envelop her being, leading to attaching and creating a meaning to the story. In this particular example, the child may attach various meanings, such as, *'I am not important. I feel abandoned. I am not good enough. He doesn't care about me. I never get my way.'*

These personal meanings begin to shape the lens through which the child perceives themselves and the world around them. They carry this meaning throughout their life and continue to find evidence of its truth.

Within you, there are two aspects of your inner child: *the free child and the wounded child*. The free child represents the playful, creative and joyful part of you that wants to explore and have fun. On the other hand, the wounded child is the part that carries the subconscious limiting belief system. Also known as the victim, the ego, toxicity, pain, triggers and the comfort zone, otherwise known as *trauma*.

The wounded child holds onto the stories and meanings associated with past experiences, continuously seeking further evidence throughout your life to validate those beliefs. The wounded child within you needs healing and nurturing. It is the part of you that carries pain, gets triggered by certain events or situations and requires attention and care. By acknowledging and addressing the needs of this wounded child, you can begin the process of healing. This involves understanding the traumas that have affected you, providing the support and love that the wounded child requires and working towards releasing the pain and negative beliefs associated with those experiences. These negative limiting beliefs live in the subconscious mind and most of the time we are not even aware of them. Through this healing journey, you can nurture your wounded inner child, allowing it to transform and grow into a more empowered and healed version of yourself.

Be aware that the wounded child (subconscious mind) has awe-inspiring power, and their strength and stubbornness can be both astonishing and tenacious. The subconscious mind can override the conscious mind because of this power. It possesses a remarkable ability to embrace victimhood, often finding comfort in clinging tightly to the familiar meaning of its original story, whether true or not. The wounded child clings to the profound meaning embedded within their story, persistently seeking evidence throughout their life to affirm its truth. In this chapter, we will embark upon a profound exploration of the intricacies woven within these early events, meanings and emotions through your first ten years of life. Together, we will unravel the layers of your personal narratives, shedding light upon the profound impact they have had on your life. Through this journey of self-discovery and healing, we will find inspiration and motivation to reclaim your inherent worthiness, rewrite the meanings to your stories and embrace a path of freedom and empowerment. Let's undertake this extraordinary process of transformation as we work hand in hand to reprogram your limiting beliefs. Brace yourself to rediscover the radiant and dynamic essence of your free child, the part of you that is vibrant, powerful and joyfully playful.

In the early stages of our lives, pivotal moments of wounding lay the foundation for our responses and behaviours, mirroring the beliefs we hold about ourselves. These initial wounds shape our perception of self and influence the circumstances we attract into our lives, providing evidence that reinforces our deeply ingrained narratives and self-value. Unbeknownst to our conscious awareness, we continually seek out various pieces of evidence that align with these beliefs. Our experiences, like magnets, draw forth situations that validate our internalised stories. This pattern operates within our unconscious realm, exerting its influence until we awaken to the power of awareness and understanding. Once we gain clarity and comprehension, we transcend the cycle of repetition. With newfound consciousness, we can identify the unhealed aspects residing within us. This serves as the catalyst for commencing a transformative journey of healing and reprogramming. By bravely venturing into the depths of our being, we uncover the wounds that have long lain hidden. Through the process of healing, we rewrite the narratives that have shaped our lives to free ourselves from the past and old patterns, as we pave the way to bring forth liberation and the reclamation of our truest selves.

First, you must identify that the wounded child has three distinct aspects that shape their perception of the world. Each of these aspects plays a vital role in shaping your responses to life's unfolding events and your expectations of what lies ahead. They converge together to form the lens through which you perceive the world and determine what you believe life will deliver to you.

The first aspect is our **childhood wounding**. This is a collection of traumas and experiences that leave a lasting impact on our young souls. The negative impact we carry from our past experiences stems from the interpretations our inner child placed upon those stories. These stories are deeply personal, representing the narratives of our individual journeys and the emotional reactions we held onto in our memories until this very day. These wounds become woven into the fabric of our being, influencing the narratives we construct and the meanings we assign to our stories. They become the foundation upon which our responses to life are built. This unique blend of experiences, and the meanings we attach to them, becomes the foundation from which we navigate our present reality. It serves as a compass, influencing our choices, actions and emotional responses. Yet, within the depths of these wounds lies the potential for extraordinary healing and transformation. By exploring and reprogramming these past wounds, we liberate ourselves from their grip and open the door to new possibilities.

The second aspect is **our observation,** the keen eye through which we perceive and make sense of the world around us. It is through our observations that we acquire a deep understanding of what is deemed to be true. Our young minds absorb the beliefs, behaviours and patterns exhibited by those around us, especially our parents, imprinting them within our psyche. These observations become the building blocks of our own belief systems. They shape our understanding as we absorb the beliefs, values and limitations of those around us. However, within this awareness also lies the opportunity to discern and question the validity of these inherited perspectives. By consciously choosing to expand our observation beyond the confines of our conditioned thinking, we unlock the potential for new insights and fresh possibilities.

The third aspect is **our ancestral DNA,** the profound influence of our family lineage, carrying within it the imprints of deep wounds passed down through generations. These ancestral traumas ripple through time, leaving an indelible mark on our collective consciousness. They shape our energy, beliefs and values, manifesting in familial and cultural dynamics, stories, language and rituals. We become inheritors of these ancestral imprints, carrying them within us and navigating their impact on our lives. Our ancestral DNA serves as a silent influence on our perceptions and expectations. The energy and beliefs surrounding family and cultural wounds are etched into our being, shaping our experiences and colouring our outlook. Yet within this inheritance, there is also an invitation to examine and transcend the limitations that may have been passed down. By fearlessly examining our ancestral lineage with curiosity and compassion, we can heal ancestral wounds and rewrite the narratives that have bound us.

Recognising the interplay of these aspects offers us a remarkable opportunity for growth, expansion and transformation. It inspires us to embark on a journey of self-mastery where we cultivate the awareness to recognise the conditioned responses and expectations that may hold us back. We empower ourselves to rewrite the script, thus creating new narratives that align with our deepest desires and aspirations. Through this exploration, we release the untapped potential within us, igniting a flame of inspiration and motivation. We realise that we have the power to transcend the limitations imposed by our conditioning and to shape our own destinies. It is within our hands to respond to life's events in a way that aligns with our truest selves, to create new possibilities and embrace a life that exceeds our highest expectations.

In this realisation, we discover that our journey is not only one of personal growth and fulfilment, but also a contribution to the collective consciousness. As we embrace the power of conscious response and release ourselves from the shackles of conditioned expectations, we become beacons of inspiration for others. Our transformative journey becomes a testament to the human spirit and an invitation for all to step into their own power and rewrite their stories.

It becomes evident that the effects of our childhood programming, our observations and ancestral heritage run deep. However, within this very realisation lies the power to transcend and transform. By delving into the depths of our being, we can unravel the threads that bind us to old wounds and limiting beliefs. Through awareness and understanding, we gain the inspiration and motivation to heal and claim our lives. By undertaking the sacred work of healing, we not only liberate ourselves, but also contribute to the healing of our lineage and the collective consciousness. It is through this profound process of self-transformation that we reclaim our authentic power and emerge as catalysts for positive change. The journey of healing and reprogramming offers a path of expansion, expression and the ultimate liberation of our truest selves.

So, let us embark on this transformative odyssey together, unravelling the layers of conditioning, identifying the limitations of our subconscious beliefs and embracing the expansiveness of possibility and reclaiming our innate ability to shape the outcomes of our lives.

May your exploration be infused with expression, inspiration and motivation as you unlock the extraordinary potential that resides within you. Now, let us travel into the depths of your childhood, where the earliest seeds of conditioning were sown. Take a moment to transport yourself back to those formative years up to the age of ten, as we access the power of your earliest memories. Recall the first story that etched itself into your being, leaving behind a trace of negativity—whether it be sadness, anger, confusion, or when things simply didn't go your way, leaving you with a negative impact.

These stories need not be one of intense trauma, but can often be a seemingly small tale that impacted your perception of self in some way. It is within these moments that you will discover the building blocks of your conditioned responses. So, with gentle introspection, let the memory surface and fill your consciousness. As the memory dances before your mind's eye, turn your attention to the meaning you attached to these stories. With discovering the list of these meanings, your understanding of self and the world deepens. It is through these interpretations that you navigate your reality, influencing the choices you make, the relationships you form and the paths you walk. As you unravel the layers of these meanings, you gain insight into the patterns that have shaped your life. You begin to see how these interpretations have impacted your experiences, influencing your thoughts, emotions and actions. As you shine the light of awareness upon them, you create space for new possibilities to emerge.

I now invite you to embrace the expansiveness of your being. For within the richness of your interpretations lies the power to take control of your subconscious mind. Through introspection and self-reflection, you can peel back the layers of conditioning and uncover the truths that resonate with your authentic self. It is in this act of unravelling that you find the seeds of inspiration and motivation. You realise that you possess the power to redefine your stories, to infuse them with empowering meanings that align with your highest aspirations. Each layer you peel back brings you closer to reclaiming your innate worth, unlocking the extraordinary potential that resides within you.

Let us take this transformative journey together, for it is through the exploration of our earliest stories and the meanings we attach to them that we reclaim our power to shape our lives. With courage and curiosity, we embrace the expansion of self-expression and the liberation of our truest essence.

In the next exercise, you will be asked to enter a sacred space of self-reflection where you will take a moment to reconnect with your memories and allow the stories to flow.

Begin by remembering the first story that comes to your awareness that left a negative impact on your young self. Dive deep into the depths of your consciousness and recall the memory, feeling the emotions of this pivotal moment. Begin to write down these memories. These stories are like fragments of a kaleidoscope, constantly shifting and revealing new facets of your being. With each story that surfaces, honour its presence. Whether you recall one story or many, know that each holds a key to unlocking the hidden meanings that have shaped your life so far.

This exercise is of utmost importance, as it serves as a foundation for your formula of transformation. These stories, laden with their unique meanings, will accompany you throughout this sacred process. They will guide you as you navigate the intricate pathways of healing and growth. Allow the words to flow from your pen as you note down these stories, your response to them and the meaning you placed on them. Embrace the vulnerability of this process, for it is within the depths of our stories that we discover the raw truths of our existence. Do it without judgment or expectation.

Take this moment to immerse yourself in the first ten years of your life. As you undertake this process, you will discover the meaning you attach to each story. Know that by honestly evaluating these stories, you are embarking on a vital process of self-transformation. Remember, these stories can be small and seem insignificant at first. Not all will be deep, painful narratives.

This exercise will guide you to lay the groundwork for a deeper understanding of yourself and the intricate web of limited subconscious beliefs that have shaped your reality. As you reflect upon these stories, you open the door to reprogramming your trauma, infusing them with empowering meanings that resonate with your true essence. This is the beginning of a remarkable journey—one that will lead you to greater self-awareness, healing and growth. Approach this exercise with an open heart and a willingness to explore the depths of your being. Trust in the process, for within it lies the power to reclaim your authentic self and create a life aligned with your deepest desires. May this exercise be a catalyst for intense self-discovery, igniting the spark of inspiration and motivation within you. Embrace the transformative power of your stories and the meanings they hold, for they are the beautiful threads that weave the tapestry of your life. You are a step closer to unlocking the boundless potential that resides within you. Embrace this sacred process of self-exploration and allow it to guide you towards a life of purpose and fulfilment. Let your stories unfold and pave your way.

Here's one example I can share from my life.

My first memory to cast a shadow of negativity upon my childhood was at the age of three. I remember I was in my aunt's house, where porcelain dolls sat on top of her kitchen cupboards. I asked if I could play with them, only to be met with a heart-wrenching rejection. In that moment, sadness and frustration engulfed me, tears streaming down my cheeks. Little did I know the meanings I attributed in that moment to this simple story would hold truth within me for years to come. Through the innocent lens of my young, inexperienced self, the meanings I put to this story was, *'I don't get what I want. I'm not trusted. I am not worth. I'm not important.'*

These deeply ingrained meanings birthed a powerful narrative that reverberated within the depths of my subconscious, intricately shaping my perceptions regarding my self-worth. Persistently resurfacing, these meanings presented themselves as evidence, casting shadows throughout my life.

It wasn't until I fully committed myself to this inner work and the transformative process of reprogramming that I truly understood the depth of my own power. I realised that I had the ability to transcend my limiting self-beliefs, paving the way for empowering truths. By challenging and reframing these limiting beliefs, I liberated myself from their grip, unveiling a newfound sense of confidence and aligning with who I really am.

This is the beginning. This heartfelt activity will help you unravel the depths of your subconscious mind and the intricate web of your emotional responses, the meanings you put to your stories and the lies you have told yourself for years. It is through this process that you can reclaim your power, redefine your self-perception and create a life aligned with your true desires. Trust in your ability to uncover the wisdom within you. This exercise is a catalyst for growth, expansion and transformation. Allow yourself to fully engage with it and be open to the unlimited possibilities that await you. Freely write down every story that comes to you and allow yourself the time to uncover its significance in your life. Embrace this exercise as a gateway to personal empowerment and the reclamation of your true self—not the wounded child's truth.

In each column, you will explore the interplay between the events that have shaped your life, your emotional reactions to those events and the meanings you (the inner child) have constructed around them. Begin by recalling the stories that left a negative impact on you as a child up to the age of ten. Next to each story, write down the emotional reaction you had to that story, and in the last column write down the meaning the young you attached to the story.

EXERCISE
Discovering Childhood Wounding

EVENT: (Story that gave you a negative impact)	RESPONSE: (Emotional reaction)	MEANING: (The meaning that the child attatched to the story)
E.g. 3 years old: My Aunty wouldn't let me play with her dolls.	Sad Frustrated Irritated	I don't get what I want I'm not trusted I am not worthy I'm not important

EVENT: (Story that gave you a negative impact)	RESPONSE: (Emotional reaction)	MEANING: (The meaning that the child attatched to the story)

By completing this exercise, you will notice some valuable insights into the meanings you have given the stories that have influenced your thoughts, emotions and actions. This awareness will empower you to challenge and rewrite these meanings, freeing yourself from limiting beliefs and embracing a more empowering perspective. Remember, this exercise is the first big stepping stone on your journey to become aware of your subconscious thoughts. You may discover that the meanings you assigned to the stories in your childhood have been repeating through your life and trying to find evidence that they are true.

By identifying these connections, you can begin to unravel the deeply ingrained patterns that shape your adult experiences. Allow this process to serve as a catalyst for rebooting your memory and unearthing similar stories from your childhood. The meanings you attached to events in your past are likely being echoed in your present, reinforcing certain beliefs and expectations. It is your responsibility now to release the childhood meanings you have attached to your self-worth and how you see the world. The feelings you had during these childhood events are valid, however your subconscious doesn't need to keep finding evidence of them in your adult life. At the heart of your traumas lies a core essence, representing deeply ingrained themes that have shaped your experiences. These themes act as emotional triggers throughout your life, resurfacing in various situations and stimulating similar reactions to those you had as a child. In these moments, you find yourself revisiting the same meanings and beliefs that were established by the wounded child within you.

These triggers may evoke intense emotions and activate automatic responses that mirror the patterns of the past. They create a powerful link between present circumstances and any unresolved pain from earlier experiences. The wounded child's perspective takes hold, leading you to interpret events through the lens of past traumas and reinforcing the narratives you have carried for so long. Recognising these triggers and the repetitive nature of your reactions is a crucial step towards healing and transformation. By bringing awareness to these patterns, you can begin to disentangle yourself from the grip of the wounded child's beliefs and reclaim your power over your reactions. This process allows you to begin responding to your life experiences rather than reacting like you have in the past.

You have the power to reprogram your subconscious mind and reshape your current reality. By identifying and understanding the origins of your limiting beliefs, you can liberate yourself from this grip and forge a new path ahead. You can now reconnect with your past, drawing wisdom from the stories that have shaped you. By doing so, you create fresh space for growth, healing and transformation. With each revelation, you move closer to liberating yourself from the limitations of the conscious mind and bringing it into the limitless beliefs of your conscious mind.

May this exploration rekindle your memory and ignite a profound understanding of how your early experiences have influenced your present reality. Trust in your ability to uncover the threads that connect your past and present, for within them lie the keys to unlocking your true potential. As this principle dives into the depths of your past, it uncovers the layers of meaning that have shaped your adult experiences. By shedding light on the connections between your childhood meanings and your current lived reality, you empower yourself to break free from the patterns that no longer serve you.

With an open heart let the revelations guide you towards a life of authenticity, self-compassion and empowerment. Your capacity to rewrite your story begins now. Now that we have become aware of the narratives you formed in childhood, it's time you look deeper and unravel their intricate layers.

Now begin to weave together instances from your present life that align with the beliefs you hold about yourself and the recurring patterns you perceive. You may notice that the wounded child within you seeks validation for the truth of these narratives. It actively creates situations and circumstances that reinforce the meaning of your childhood stories. However, it is the responsibility of your adult self, guided by your higher self, to embark on a journey of healing and transformation.

Through this process, you can restore harmony within by tending to the wounded inner child with kindness and clarity. By doing so, you pave the way for your new worldview—one that is infused with freedom and infinite possibilities. Direct your attention to your relationships and the events, both past and present, that have unfolded in your life. Are the meanings you assigned as a child still resonant, echoing through your present experiences? Do the associated narratives tied to these recurring meanings continue to manifest in your adult life? By honestly investigating these connections, you will gain insight into the ways in which your childhood beliefs have influenced the course of your life. This awareness empowers you to question, challenge and ultimately transcend the limitations imposed by these ingrained meanings. It is through this process of introspection and reflection that you reclaim your personal power and open the doors to new limitless beliefs.

As you untangle the web of patterns through conscious exploration and deliberate choices, you create the space for growth and the emergence of new possibilities. This is an invitation to examine the connection between your childhood meanings and your present reality. By doing so, you unlock the potential to rewrite your story, reclaim your inherent worth and shape a future filled with abundance, fulfilment and joy. Trust in your capacity to create a new narrative—one that reflects your true essence and propels you towards a life of purpose and authenticity. The choice to redefine your reality begins now.

Have the revelations you have uncovered surprised you? Have you made the profound connection between the thoughts of the wounded child within you and the unconscious creations that have permeated your entire life? It's a moment of realisation, isn't it?

In this moment of clarity, you may have just discovered that you have been perpetuating these meanings and narratives throughout your existence. I want to remind you that it is all based on a lie—a distorted perception formed in the incomplete picture of your childhood experiences. As children, we lack the emotional intelligence and depth of understanding to grasp the truth in its entirety. We are still in the process of navigating the complexities of our world and finding our place within it. In our early years, we rely on others to define who we are, to fulfil our needs and to provide love and acceptance.

When we encounter rejection or perceive it, even if it is seemingly insignificant, the wounded child within us feels the sting. It is in these moments of perceived abandonment or rejection that the seeds of our wounds are sown. The child's dependence on others for validation and a sense of self leaves them vulnerable to these wounds. But here's the truth: the wounded child's interpretation of events is not the complete truth. It is an interpretation coloured by our limited understanding and the perspective of a developing mind. As adults, we have the power to see beyond the narrow lens of the wounded child and embrace a broader, more conscious understanding of our experiences. Through this exploration, we shed light on the false meanings we have told ourselves, and now it's time to embody our greater truth.

It is within your power to challenge the lies that have held you captive and to embrace a more expansive, empowering narrative. This is your process to reclaim your autonomy and sense of self. Recognise that you no longer need to rely solely on others to define your worth or shape your reality. You have the power within you to nurture, heal yourself and rewrite the script of your life. You do not need validation from others. If anything, it's your wounded child you need to validate and nurture and only you can do that by healing, reprogramming and awakening to your true potential. This revelation is a valuable opportunity for self-compassion and forgiveness. Extend understanding to the wounded child within you, knowing that they acted from a place of limited awareness and survival.

You are not bound by the wounds of the past. You have the capacity to transcend them, to release the grip of the wounded child's narratives and to create a life that reflects your innate worth and potential. The power to rewrite your story lies within you, awaiting your courageous acceptance. Let the knowledge that you are not defined by the wounds of your past ignite a fire within you—a fire fuelled by self-compassion, resilience and the unwavering belief in your ability to create a life of joy and truth. You possess the power to transform your beliefs and create new narratives that align with your true potential and highest aspirations. Reprogramming begins with a conscious choice—a choice to release the old, limiting beliefs and allow the conscious mind to replace them with empowering ones. It requires consistent effort, practise and repetition. As you navigate this process, remember that this journey will take time. To reprogram your meanings starts by questioning their truth. Are they serving your highest good? Do they align with the person you aspire to become? Challenge the beliefs that hold you back and open yourself to new possibilities.

Affirmations and positive self-talk play a vital role in the reprogramming process. Engaging in daily affirmations reinforces new meanings that you want to embody. Repeat affirmations with conviction, feeling their positive energy penetrating your mind and body, and claiming them as your new vibration of truth. Remember, reprogramming is not an overnight process. It requires daily patience and perseverance. Be gentle with yourself as you navigate the ups and downs of the reprogramming. Celebrate even the smallest victories and milestones you feel along the way, for they are significant indicators of your progress. The more you confirm your new beliefs, the more you start to see within your reality the physical evidence of the new means you are creating. As you reprogram, feel yourself embodying the new meanings that empower and uplift you. See yourself embracing opportunities, manifesting abundance and cultivating deep fulfilment in all areas of your life. Let this vision inspire and motivate you to stay committed to your new reprogramming practice.

In moments of doubt or setbacks, be patient and trust in your ability to rewrite the meanings you gave your stories and create a new reality that aligns with your authentic self. Embrace the power of choice and intention as you bring it into your consciousness. Reprogramming is a radical act of self-love and empowerment. It is a declaration that you are the author of your own life, capable of rewriting the narratives that shape your reality.

In this following exercise, we focus on reprogramming the meanings you have identified and affirming their empowering opposites. By consciously shifting your beliefs, you can create a new mindset that supports your growth and wellbeing.

Some examples:
Limiting belief: *I don't get what I want.*
Becomes the new belief: *I get what I want.*
Limiting belief: *I am not good enough.*
Becomes the new belief: *I am enough.*

In the following exercise, you will create your own new beliefs. Creating new affirmations for you to reinforce daily as many times as you can reminds you that you have the power to manifest your desires and attract what you want into your life. Imagine yourself with unwavering confidence, effortlessly attaining your goals and receiving the desires of your heart. It's not merely a matter of speaking affirmations; it's about truly embodying them, feeling them, believing in them with every cell in your body and allowing their essence to permeate the depths of your soul as if you already possess them. Reprogram them from the limiting belief system to a new and improved belief system. Feel it with every fibre of your being, convincing your mind, body and cells that this is the undeniable truth. By embracing this new reality, you unleash a powerful force within yourself that propels you towards manifesting your aspirations and creating a life filled with abundance and joy.

These new empowering beliefs are a gentle daily reminder of the inherent worth and value that resides within you. Allow them to serve as a guiding light, illuminating the path towards self-acceptance and recognising the unique qualities that make you truly remarkable. Let these new beliefs nurture a deep sense of confidence and appreciation for your own worthiness. Recognise that you are deserving of love, success and happiness just as you are. Celebrate your unique qualities and strengths and let go of self-judgment and comparison.

As you engage in this reprogramming exercise, remember to embody these beliefs with conviction. Affirmations work best when repeated consistently and in a positive emotional state. Integrate your new affirmations into your daily routine, whether through written statements, verbal repetition or visual reminders. You could put your affirmations on your mirror, the fridge or your bedside table—anywhere they will help reinforce your practice. Additionally, complement your affirmations with self-care practices and actions that reinforce your newfound beliefs. Engage in activities that nourish your self-esteem and cultivate love. Surround yourself with supportive and uplifting influences. Over time, you will witness the transformation of your beliefs and the positive impact they have on your life. You will begin to witness the evidence presenting itself into your reality from your new reprogramming beliefs. Trust in the process, remain committed and celebrate your progress along the way. Remember, you have the power to create your reality and embrace a new mindset.

In this transformative journey of reprogramming your subconscious mind, the list you've created serves as the powerful foundation for change. It's important to understand that the process of creating new habits and beliefs typically takes between twenty-one and twenty-seven days. According to neurologists, the process of reprogramming your subconscious mind typically takes approximately three to four weeks, although the timeframe may vary based on the level of ingrained behaviour and the depth of your individual limiting beliefs. The key lies in shifting the energy and thoughts you wish to attract into your life. To initiate this transformation, it is essential to make a conscious decision and wholeheartedly commit to the process. Embracing your new empowering beliefs becomes paramount, so allow them to permeate your thoughts and emotions. Cultivating a sense of gratitude, as if your desired changes have already manifested to reinforce this shift.

Finally, surrendering to the deep knowing and trusting that these changes have indeed occurred opens the door to the changes that you seek. Adopt these practices and align your mindset and feelings, knowing that you already are the changes you seek. Be in control of your thoughts. Don't let your subconscious thoughts be in control of you.

Within a relatively short timeframe, your mind can initiate a significant shift. Communicate with your body to send new instructions you can embody. This connection between the mind and body is not just a mere concept; it is a neurological and psychosomatic fact that has been scientifically validated. Consider the intricate communication between your mind and body. As your mind sends messages, your body responds by sending the same messages back, forming a circuit that alters your energetic frequency. This transformational shift in frequency becomes your new way of being, ultimately shaping your lived experience. Tap into the tremendous power within yourself to rewire your subconscious patterns and create a new life that aligns with your desired beliefs and intentions. It is a journey where you consciously choose to rewrite the script of your inner narrative.

Let us begin by filling in the table. Rewrite all your meanings (from the previous exercise) in the left column. In the right column, write down its direct opposite.

The next page shows a few examples to guide you.

EXERCISE
Reprogramming Meanings

LIST MEANINGS	AFFIRM THE OPPOSITE
E.g. I don't get what I want	I do get what I want
I'm not trusted	I am always trusted
I am not worthy	I am worthy
I'm not important	I am important

LIST MEANINGS	AFFIRM THE OPPOSITE

Now it's time to devote yourself to a focused thirty-day practice. Immerse yourself fully in this activity to strengthen and amplify your newfound beliefs. Through consistent engagement, you create a powerful vessel for transformation, allowing your new beliefs to take root and flourish within your being. This dedicated period of concentrated effort will be a catalyst for extraordinary growth and the manifestation of your desired reality. Whilst engaging in your daily affirmations, visualise your desired state of being.

As you persistently embody new beliefs, you will witness the subtle yet strong shifts taking place within you. Your mind and body will synchronise harmoniously, creating a powerful feedback loop that reinforces your new frequency. The more you immerse yourself in this process, the more natural and effortless your new way of being becomes. Be committed. Trust in the capacity of your mind and body to adapt and welcome new patterns.

With each passing day, you will notice that you react differently to familiar situations. In the past, you may have taken feedback personally or to heart as an attack on your character. With your newly formed beliefs, you will be able to see more objectively and become conscious of what the wounded child is whispering in your ear, knowing it is trying to protect you but with outdated and incorrect truth. It is your job to catch and flip those whispers, make sure you nurture the wounded child and be strong by affirming, *'I don't give you power'*, *'I am not listening to you anymore'*, *'That is not my truth'*. The wounded child is attached to your ego. When it is seen and heard by you, the conscious human, it subsides. By eliminating the wounded child, you're encouraging the behaviour of the free child to take charge.

You are the author of your own narrative and through the reprogramming of your subconscious mind, you open doors to infinite possibilities and a transformation that resonates with your deepest aspirations.

When reprogramming our subconscious mind, the key lies in the consistent repetition of these affirmations. Our subconscious mind operates on the basis of feelings, and it responds to the state of being that we cultivate within ourselves.

When we genuinely feel something to be true, it becomes our reality.

It is through our feelings that our beliefs are formed, regardless of whether they are positive or negative. By immersing ourselves in the constant repetition of affirming statements, we create a powerful shift within our subconscious mind. Taking control of our mind, instead of our subconscious mind taking control over us. We anchor ourselves in a state of belief and conviction, where the affirmations become our truth. Through this process, we gradually replace limiting beliefs and negative thought patterns with empowering and uplifting ones. Through repetition, we strengthen the neural pathways in our brain that support our new beliefs. We pave the way for a positive mindset and a renewed perspective on ourselves and the world around us. Repetition and conviction is the key that unlocks the door to lasting change. Our affirmations gain momentum and become deeply embedded in our subconscious. As we embrace the feelings and the emotional state associated with these affirmations, we align ourselves with the vibration of our desired reality.

By regularly practicing your new beliefs as affirmations, you create a clear shift in your internal landscape. Your subconscious mind begins to respond to a new feeling state you have cultivated. It becomes fertile ground for the seeds of positive beliefs to flourish and grow. Remember, the power of repetition lies in its ability to rewire your neural pathways and transform the perception of yourself and the world. This is why I recommend a thirty-day practice to give you the momentum. As you affirm your new beliefs, watch how your subconscious mind responds. Observe subtle shifts in your thoughts, emotions and behaviours. Notice how your reality starts to align with the truth you are affirming. Incorporate the power of repetition and conviction into your life and witness the profound impact it has.

You can rewrite the script of your subconscious mind. In the process of affirming these new beliefs, it is natural to encounter some initial difficulty and a sense of unfamiliarity. However, with consistent practice and dedication, your mind will gradually accept the messages you are consciously communicating to it and your body will respond accordingly. When affirming, it is essential to speak in the present tense, as if the desired state has already been achieved. By using phrases such as 'I am ...' or 'I have ...', you activate the power of the present moment and engage with the emotions associated with your desired reality. This creates a powerful alignment between your thoughts, feelings and the belief system you are cultivating.

As you persist in affirming these new beliefs with heartfelt conviction, your mind begins to internalise and adopt them. It gradually recognises them as the truth and adjusts its perception of reality accordingly. This shift in your internal landscape reverberates into your external circumstances, as your mind's acceptance of the new beliefs is reflected in the experiences and opportunities that manifest in your life. As you continue affirming your new beliefs, observe how they become increasingly ingrained in your subconscious programming. Notice how they shape your thoughts, emotions and actions. Trust in the process and in due time, your mind will fully embrace these new beliefs, allowing them to shape your experiences and create the life you envision. Affirm with conviction, feel the truth of your affirmations and welcome the transformation that unfolds as your mind aligns with the new beliefs you are consciously instilling. Embrace the power of affirmation as a catalyst for positive change and a gateway to the limitless potential within you.

During this transformative period of reprogramming, it is crucial to cultivate a heightened sense of self-awareness regarding your emotional state and any counterproductive beliefs that may arise. This journey requires time, mindfulness, and above all, patience with yourself. There is one vital rule to keep in mind: should you stumble and find yourself slipping back into the grip of your limiting beliefs, where you feel like a victim once again, you must restart the process from day one the following day. However, there is an important exception to this rule. If you catch yourself mid-fall and swiftly shift your perspective to the positive new reality, you can continue progressing without resetting. Only when you completely forget and lose awareness of your new thought patterns should you begin the thirty days again.

The mind is an immensely powerful entity, and the subconscious tends to cling to what is familiar and comfortable. It is said that we have approximately 60,000 thoughts a day and that seventy-five per cent of these thoughts are negative and ninety-five per cent are on repeat and driven by the fight-or-flight part of our brain. I am not going to lie to you. At first, this will be difficult because your subconsciousness is powerful and has established patterns since birth. It's important to remember that you are powerful and can gain control over your thoughts. With repetition, you will get results.

Throughout this process, practise self-compassion and gentleness, for you are venturing into uncharted territory—a new way of thinking that inevitably leads to a new way of being. It may feel unfamiliar at first, but I have unwavering belief in your ability to navigate this path. You possess the strength and resilience to embrace this transformation with grace. Trust in yourself, for you are capable of triumphing over any obstacles that may arise.

What is important here is that your new beliefs are a 'knowing' of having that thing already. Your beliefs have to be so precise, the frequency has to be exactly on point.

Think of something you are naturally good at. Align your new beliefs with that same feeling. I ask my clients this all the time. One of them said they are great at organising, so I asked her to align that same feeling with her new affirmations. Feel into what you are already great at. That feeling is what you want in your present reality when affirming your new beliefs.

Today marks the beginning of your transformative journey—day one of reprogramming your subconscious mind. Embrace this momentous occasion with enthusiasm and determination.

May this Day One ignite a spark within you, fuelling your determination and inspiring you to persistently pursue the reprogramming of your subconscious mind. Trust in your ability to create positive change and let the journey unfold with grace and purpose. Rely upon the power of discipline as you embark on this journey, for it is an investment in the very fabric of your existence. Celebrate this new reality in your life, for it holds the promise of a radiant future. Stay committed, stay focused and watch in awe as your dreams unfold before your eyes. The journey awaits and the free child within eagerly yearns to spread its wings and soar into a reality that knows no bounds.

As you begin this process, it is normal to encounter triggers that evoke feelings of limitation or past conditioning. In other words, be assured you will be tested, because the subconscious mind naturally wants to stay in the old comfort zone. Simply being aware and catching these triggers is a significant step in breaking free from their hold. Resist the temptation to fall back into the familiar patterns of the past, recognising that they no longer serve your highest good, and refocus on your new beliefs. When you venture into new territory and strive to create a different reality, your inner critic often emerges, attempting to discourage you. Treat yourself with kindness and compassion, acknowledging the presence of your emotions and limiting beliefs without becoming drawn back into them.

Remember, awareness without judgment allows for the release of these patterns from your consciousness. Rather than dwelling on past setbacks or perceived shortcomings, focus on the present moment and the progress you are making. Each step, no matter how small, contributes to your growth and transformation. As you progress on this path of personal growth, it is important to keep moving forwards, no matter the obstacles you encounter. Time will be your ally, providing a measure of your commitment and dedication to this process. If you find yourself slipping back into familiar patterns and old responses, refrain from being too harsh on yourself. Recognise that the programming you are endeavouring to alter has been ingrained over a lifetime. Be gentle and understanding with yourself and take the opportunity to start anew each day.

By cultivating awareness, practicing self-kindness, acknowledging your emotions and limiting beliefs without judgment, you create space for deep release and transformation. Savour the power of the present moment, allowing it to fuel your progress and propel you forwards on your journey to a new and empowering reality. Take note of the progress you have made, the lessons you have learnt and the insights you have gained. Allow these experiences to empower you, motivating you to continue your journey of reprogramming with renewed vigour. Remember, change is a gradual process that unfolds over time. In the event that you experience a break or interruption in your reprogramming practice, simply acknowledge it as a part of your unique journey. If necessary, restart the thirty-day cycle, understanding that consistency and commitment are key to achieving lasting change.

Welcome to the profound initiation into *The Formula of Life*, where the threads of our stories intertwine with the meanings we assign to them, shaping the wounded child within us. Within this formula lies the key to liberation and the emergence of the free child that resides within each of us. Every story, every experience, every event holds a unique meaning that we attach to it. These meanings become the lenses through which we perceive ourselves and the world around us. They shape our beliefs, our behaviours and ultimately the wounded child within us. It is within the depths of this wounded child that our limitations, fears and self-imposed barriers reside.

But here's the secret: the meaning we assigned to those stories, those events, those experiences are nothing more than an illusion we bought into without fully grasping the truth. It is time to unravel this deceit and embark on the journey of reprogramming.

Reprogramming begins with the conscious unravelling of those false meanings, gently peeling back the layers of deception that have held us captive for far too long. As we unveil the truth, we liberate the child within—the authentic essence of who we truly are. To reprogram ourselves is to rewrite the narratives that have defined us. It is to infuse new meanings, new beliefs, shedding light on the empowering and uplifting aspects that have been overshadowed by the trauma of the wounded child.

Through deliberate and intentional acts of self-awareness, we replace the limiting beliefs with empowering truths. With each affirmation, each intentional choice, we rewire our subconscious mind and realign ourselves with the essence of the free child. We transcend the boundaries of our past, embracing a new reality—a reality that is anchored in freedom, authenticity and boundless possibilities.

Remember, this is just the beginning—the opening stages of your metamorphosis. As you go deeper into *The Formula of Life*, you will uncover profound revelations, ignite the flame of inspiration within and awaken to the vast reservoir of potential that resides within you, to rise higher.

Claim your power, where the fusion of your story, the unravelling of false meanings and the reprogramming of your beliefs set the stage for the emerging of the free child.

You've got this, stay committed.

Positive thoughts are the compass and alignment is the path to manifesting your heart's desires in the grand design of life.

PRINCIPLE 3

POSITIVE THINKING AND CREATING ALIGNMENT

Accepting the profound truth that there exists a magnificent force beyond our comprehension, a force governed by vibration and frequency, is a gift of immeasurable value. This gift holds the key to understanding a remarkable phenomenon: *The Power of Reflection*. Within the grand tapestry of the universe, this power seamlessly weaves its way through our lives, mirroring our deepest beliefs and vibration. Basically, the energy we put out is returned to us.

Pause for a moment and let the weight of this realisation sink in. You possess the extraordinary ability to shape your reality through the lens of your beliefs. The thoughts you hold, the convictions you nurture and the vibrations you emit become the very essence that the Universe reflects back to you. Isn't it awe-inspiring to fathom that your dreams, aspirations and desires are intricately woven into the fabric of this cosmic symphony? You hold within you the power to manifest and attract the life you envision. The Universe, with its infinite wisdom, stands ready to align with your deepest truths, amplifying your journey and guiding you towards the manifestation of your desires.

Your thoughts, beliefs and intentions shape the vibrational tapestry of your existence. By nurturing a steadfast belief in your dreams and desires, you open the floodgates of infinite possibilities. So, dare to dream big. Cultivate a fertile garden of positive thoughts and beliefs, nourishing the seeds of your desires. Trust in the vast, unseen forces that work tirelessly to support your journey. Align your frequencies with the grand tapestry of the Universe and witness the miraculous reflection of your own truths. Here you'll go even deeper and rise higher.

Know that you are a co-creator of your destiny, a harmonious participant in the symphony of life. By nurturing the power within you, you allow yourself to be guided towards a reality that resonates with your deepest desires. Think of the connection between you and the Universe like a powerful magnet. Everything you feel and think sends signals to the Universe and those signals influence what happens in your life. With this sacred wisdom, I want you to realise the incredible potential that lies within you. The Universe is like a mirror that reflects your thoughts, but here's the crucial part: it doesn't just reflect the positive aspects; it reflects *everything* you think. It tunes into the specific thoughts you have, whether they're positive or not. In essence, your thoughts and feelings have a direct impact on the reality you experience.

Let me share with you a profound revelation about the workings of the Universe. It doesn't operate solely on the basis of our spoken words; it is attuned to the vibrations carried by each word we utter. Yes, you read it right—the Universe responds to the very frequency of our words. Consider this: the phrase 'I trust' holds within it a vibrant energy, a higher frequency that resonates throughout our being. On the other hand, when we introduce the word 'don't' and say, 'I don't trust,' the entire vibrational landscape shifts, because every word has a vibration. The frequency of these words dips to a lower vibration, altering the energy that courses through us. It is remarkable to realise that a simple word like 'don't' can wield such transformative power. Its inclusion or omission has the potential to shape our entire life experience. You see, this frequency reverberates within our very essence and the Universe, in its infinite wisdom, aligns us with experiences and manifestations that are in harmony with that frequency.

So, be mindful of the words you choose. Let your language be a vessel for uplifting vibrations that resonate with the life you wish to create. By consciously infusing your thoughts and feelings with positive energy, you set in motion a magnetic pull towards experiences that align with your elevated frequency. Remember, you are the orchestrator of your vibrational symphony. Your words hold the power to shape the energetic landscape of your existence. With each thought and feeling, you are weaving a tapestry of resonance that attracts circumstances, opportunities and people who vibrate at a similar frequency. Embrace this understanding with open arms, for it empowers you to take charge of your reality. Let the frequency of your words and emotions soar to the highest realms, inviting into your life a harmonious chorus of abundance, love and fulfilment. Be mindful of the subtle shifts that occur when you choose words of empowerment and positivity, for they have the potential to reshape the entire fabric of your being.

You must unleash the power of your thoughts and feelings whilst witness the miraculous dance of manifestation that unfolds. Enjoy the beauty of resonance and align yourself with the frequencies that match your deepest desires. With each uttered phrase, you immerse yourself in the symphony of creation, as the Universe conspires to bring forth the manifestations that echo your elevated vibration. Believe in the transformative potential that lies within your very speech, for it has the ability to shape your destiny. Let your words become a force that propels you towards a life of boundless joy, love and abundance. The Universe eagerly listens, responding to the vibrations you send out, as you co-create a reality that aligns with your highest aspirations.

Let's explore the concept of vibration and frequency more closely. Everything, including our bodies, vibrates at a specific frequency. Our emotions generate energy that resonates with the universe. Emotions are essentially energy in motion. We can decide which energetic frequency we want to align with and project. Guilt and shame are low-frequency energies, while joy and peace are high-frequency energies.

Every frequency has a rate in which current changes direction per second. It is measured in hertz (Hz). One hertz is equal to one cycle per second. A cycle is one complete wave of alternating current or voltage. The lower the frequency, the fewer the oscillations (movement back and forth in regular rhythm). High frequency produce more oscillations. The higher the hertz the higher the vibration. Hertz above 400 helps reduce stress and increase concentration and promote deep states of relaxation in the mind and body. These effects are the result of neurological reactions to the harmonic vibrations. 432 hertz Hz has gained importance in music therapy because it can help with releasing emotional blockages and support the healing process.

Every form of matter vibrates at a certain frequency. If you choose love and joy, you'll attract people, situations and things with that same frequency. Whatever your focused upon seems to magically arrive without effort into your life. On the other hand, if you choose fear, anger, guilt, you'll attract people, situations and things that match that vibration. Here's a simple chart that shows common emotions and their associated vibrational frequency.

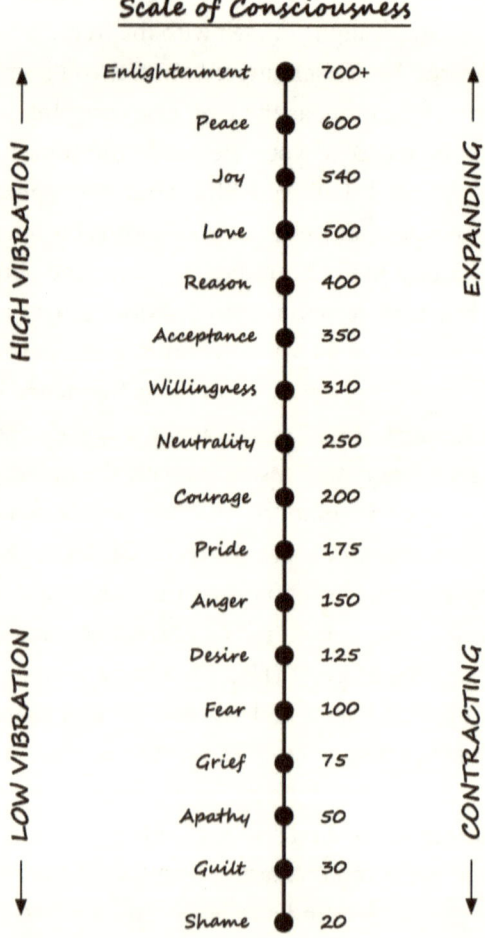

Just like you can tune into a specific radio station, you need to be exact on the frequency to hear the sound clearly. Similarly, you need to align with the exact vibrational frequency to manifest the life you desire. It's in a high vibration state that you can attract what you truly want. By elevating your emotional frequency to a higher vibration, you can bring your desires to life. Have you ever walked into a room and felt a heaviness or sadness? Or woke up feeling happy and grateful, noticing that everything seems to go your way during the day? These are examples of energy in motion (emotion). You're sensing the vibrational frequencies in the space around you. Being aware of your own energy helps you attract similar energy into your life. On the other hand, being unaware or unconscious of your energy might lead you to attract results you don't want.

Biologically, our brains do not know the difference between an event actually happening or the thought of the event happening. This is a helpful insight because a simple way to raise your vibration is to act and feel *as if* what you desire is already true. By truly believing and feeling that we already have what we desire, we resonate with that desired vibration and attract it into our reality.

This approach works well for improving our emotional state. Act *as if* you're in a high vibrational frequency, and you'll see everything around you start to align with it. Having said this, I know it can be sometimes difficult to make the leap from lower frequencies to higher ones. So, here's a quick tip to elevate your vibration: start by completing this simple statement:

"I like the feeling of..."

Start by tuning into the feelings in your body and mind. Repeat this exercise regularly, filling in the blank with things you enjoy and desire. (e.g., I like the feeling of peace, I like the feeling of financial freedom, I like the feeling of walking through my beautiful home, etc.). Be consistent and choose feelings like joy and peace that you want to embody. By doing this, you create a positive cycle for yourself. With practice and commitment, you can consciously access emotions that uplift you.

A great affirmation to repeat at least three times a day is:
'I am in vibrational alignment with my higher, most receptive self.'
Notice when you like what you're thinking and feeling, and when you don't. Recognise that you have control over your emotional state; it doesn't control you. A great way to start your day in the morning is by directing your energy positively. Set yourself up for progress, forward motion and mindfulness to connect with your higher self and desired vibrational frequency. Choosing new, uplifting thoughts becomes easier with practice, eventually becoming second nature.

Let me share with you a dynamic truth that can transform your life. It's a simple yet extraordinary principle called the *'Law of Attraction'*. In its essence lies the key to unlocking the abundance you seek. Here's the thing: whatever you say, whatever you feel, whether it's about yourself or the world around you, it sends a powerful message to the Universe. It's like shining a radiant energy into the cosmos, summoning forth experiences and circumstances that resonate with that exact vibration back to you. You see, the Law of Attraction operates on a principle as old as time itself: *like attracts like.* The vibrations you embody and the thoughts you hold within your heart become magnetic forces, drawing into your reality reflections of the energy you project.

Your feelings, your beliefs, your words—they all serve as messengers to the Universe, broadcasting your desires and intentions. With each thought, each expression of emotion, you are shaping the energetic currents that surround you. So, be mindful of the energy you send out. You have the power within you to consciously choose thoughts and feelings that align with your greatest aspirations. By focusing on positivity, love and abundance, you set in motion a powerful ripple effect that resonates with the Universe's grand design. Remember, the Universe is always conspiring in your favour. But what are you favouring? Is it positive or negative? As you embrace the Law of Attraction, you begin to recognise the immense influence you hold over your own reality. You begin to understand that you hold the key to bring in what you think and feel. So, it's time to bring your dreams into fruition and to believe that positive endless possibilities await you.

Start by trusting that the Universe, in its infinite wisdom, hears your call. It collaborates with the cosmic symphony to bring forth experiences and opportunities that match your vibrational frequency. By aligning your thoughts, emotions and actions with the life you desire, you become a co-creator of your own destiny. By embracing the beauty of this truth, you allow it to infuse your life with positivity and intention. Remember that everything is a choice: how you feel, act and respond. It's all a choice. Choose thoughts and feelings that lift your spirit and affirm your dreams. Speak words of empowerment and possibility. Feel the joy that arises when you align with the energy of your desires. Speak and think with positivity and wonder. In this magical dance of attraction, you become a magnet for all that you seek. As you radiate love, gratitude and abundance, the Universe responds with open arms, showering you with blessings beyond measure. Believe in the power of the Law of Attraction and watch as your reality transforms into a vibrant tapestry of fulfilment, joy and boundless possibilities.

Remember, you possess the key to unlock the door to a life of your dreams. Embrace the Law of Attraction and allow its guiding principles to illuminate your path towards a future brimming with abundance and limitless potential. It's a secret whispered by countless spiritual teachers throughout the ages, urging us to harness the immense power within our thoughts and words. Allow me to shed light on this transformative wisdom that can shape the very fabric of your existence. You see, the key lies in being mindful—mindful of what you think, mindful of what you say and mindful of how you vibrate. Every thought that arises within you, every word that escapes your lips, every feeling you carry deep in your soul carries a potent energy that ripples throughout the Universe. It is through this energy that you manifest the life you desire. It's the frequency of these thoughts and feelings that the Universe collects and reflects exactly that vibration right back to you. This is creating alignment.

Pause for a moment and observe the thoughts that dance through your mind. Are they aligned with your deepest desires and aspirations? Or do they hinder your progress, holding you back from embracing the abundance that awaits? As already mentioned, they say we have on average about 60,000 thoughts a day, but what is concerning is that seventy-five per cent of these thoughts are negative and ninety-five per cent are repetitive. We are creatures of habit and like to stay in the comfort zone, too afraid to take risks. We fear the unknown. Most people don't even know what they are thinking. I always say, 'Show me your life and I will tell you what you are thinking!' Many of my clients struggle to understand why they are creating drama or chaos or uneasiness in their life. And I will always tell them that it's because that's what they think and feel to be true.

Take, for example, a client of mine who had been single for four years without understanding why she couldn't find a nice man to share her life with. To help her, I delved deep into her thoughts and her perceptions of men. She connected everything to her ex-boyfriend, describing him as selfish and inconsiderate. Her desire was to meet a man who was kind and put her first. I wanted to know if she knew what that felt like and her response was negative. She hadn't truly experienced a kind man before and found out it stemmed back to her father in her childhood programming years. It became clear that the problem lay in her beliefs and the lingering pain from her past relationships. Her vibration was filled with fear, believing that she wouldn't meet the right man and that she wasn't good enough for a kind partner. My mission was to help her clear these negative subconscious beliefs and start afresh. I advised her to send out vibrations to the Universe that conveyed her worthiness of a kind and wonderful man entering her life. The challenge was that she didn't know how that would feel, which is where imagination comes into play—you need to 'pretend' or 'fake it till you make it.' We imagined scenarios where knew such a man and how she would feel in those moments. Much like a child playing 'mummies and daddies' and genuinely feeling the role they played, she had to authentically imagine her desired scenario. She needed to do the work and be conscious every day to put effort into this new vibration.

'Watch all the places kind, beautiful men enter your reality,' I told her. 'Even if it's the sales assistant at the fruit shop wanting to carry your shopping to the car. Collect evidence supporting where this vibration is true to you.' Once she aligned that positive frequency to her thoughts and feelings, the Universe recognised the vibrational shift and reflected her desires right back at her. She practised diligently and put in the work. When I saw her again six months later, she had met an incredible man online and had already been on several dates with him. Their vibrations matched. He was calm and patient, and she was delighted with the results. She created alignment and witnessed the evidence of her desired outcome.

With this newfound awareness, you hold the power to shape your reality. Choose to redirect your thoughts and feelings towards positivity and align with the very frequency of that vibration. Feel like it's already happened. Let go of limiting beliefs and replace them with empowering affirmations that resonate with your soul. As you shift your thoughts and words, you initiate a powerful process of manifestation. You become a conscious creator, weaving a tapestry of your desires into the very fabric of your existence. By aligning your inner world with your outer aspirations, you pave the way for the Universe to respond in kind. Trust in this process. Believe with unwavering faith that as you align your thoughts and feelings with your deepest desires, the Universe works to bring them into fruition. It's not spiritual woo-woo. It's physics! The energy you hold becomes a magnetic force, attracting experiences, opportunities and people that resonate with your desires. It's you creating alignment alongside your positive thoughts.

This is the transformative power of mindfulness and, as you begin to do the work, within a short amount of time, your reality unfolds in harmony with your intentions. I practise every day and as time goes by, it is easier and quicker as I bring my manifestations into reality. It is all because I am aware of my thoughts and feelings and deliberately align them to a positive high vibration.

Let me share another example with you. I recently conducted *The Formula of Life* course in Byron Bay, NSW, where I introduced this particular principle. I asked each participant in the class to manifest something they'd wanted for a long time but hadn't yet received. They were to be open to receiving it, align their thoughts and feelings with the desired outcome and bring it into reality within twenty-four hours. I suggested they choose something simple to test the process. The following day, I inquired about their progress and whether they had achieved their desires within the twenty-four-hour window. When I reached one particular participant, she responded, 'I wanted to see a kookaburra, but I didn't see one.' I probed further, trying to understand why she believed it hadn't happened. She explained, 'Ever since I've been in Byron Bay, I know there are so many kookaburras here, but I still haven't seen one. In Melbourne, where I used to live, I would see them all the time.' At that moment, it became clear that her own belief was blocking her manifestation. She had been telling the Universe, 'I used to see them all the time, but now I don't see them anymore.' Her vibration was sending this message and as a result, the Universe was reflecting that back to her. It's important to remember that the Universe doesn't understand words but rather the vibrations of your thoughts and feelings. If your words are saying one thing, but your body is saying another, the Universe will cancel it out. You have to create alignment between your words, your thoughts and your feelings with the exact frequency of having that wanting and then the Universe will respond desirably—if you believe it won't happen, it won't. If you believe it already has, it will appear.

I decided to take on this exact manifestation challenge for myself to demonstrate how the process functions and to prove to the class that this concept is one hundred per cent true. It's important to note that you can't control when the Universe delivers your desires; you must remain patient and trust in divine timing, surrendering to the outcome. Five days later, after returning home from the course, I was sitting in my backyard. I looked to my right and there, perched on the fence, was a kookaburra. I quickly captured a video and sent it to all the participants to illustrate the outcome. They were astonished and so excited at the results. When you are fully embracing the concept of your thoughts and feelings being perfectly aligned with your vibration, you have the power to bring anything you desire into your reality. The key to success in this manifestation was that my vibration was perfectly aligned with my thoughts and feelings, and this provided compelling evidence of how the process can yield desired results. The entire time, I imagined that I had already seen the kookaburra and therefore, I sent out gratefulness to the Universe like it had already happened. Feeling like you have already obtained the things you desire is the pivotal point of attraction. To become a master at bringing in all you desire into your reality, you must continuously and consciously practise. Every day, be mindful of your words, your thoughts, your feelings and your vibration. Let them be the seeds of your future, sown with intention and love. Take satisfaction in the empowering knowledge that you have the ability to shape your reality. With each positive thought, with each uplifting feeling, you manifest the life you desire. It's the Law of the Universe. Take this wisdom to heart and let it guide you on the path of abundance, joy and fulfilment. You have the incredible potential that lies within you. Be mindful, be intentional and watch as your dreams blossom into magnificent realities. Your thoughts hold incredible creative power. And here's the key: it all begins with awareness. Being aware means catching those negative thoughts as they arise and transforming them into positive ones. It takes practice, but it's a transformative practice that enables you to cultivate a life filled with joy and abundance. Catching your thoughts so you can continue to grow is the greatest gift to self.

One of the negative thoughts I see repeatedly amongst my clients is one with money. This is not only limited to sessions in my healing room. Many people in society at large struggle with the immense pressure and difficulties surrounding finances. The overwhelming pressure of financial difficulties is huge. The challenge arises when individuals fail to acknowledge the Universe's boundless supply of abundance. This happens due to repetitive thoughts like, 'I don't have enough money', 'That costs too much', 'I can't afford it', or 'I don't deserve it', among other limiting beliefs. This is why it's so important to reprogram those subconscious thoughts of the wounded child, as some of them will relate to this directly. Did you have meaning related to 'I'm not good enough', 'I'm not worthy', 'I don't deserve it' or 'I don't feel safe' in your childhood programming? If you resonate with these negative meanings, these patterns might be deeply ingrained in your subconscious and your body at a cellular level, affecting your ability to manifest abundance. Remember your subconscious thoughts will override the conscious thoughts every time because they are stronger. That's why it's crucial to reprogram those negative limiting beliefs. The most important missing link to manifesting is the necessity to clearing the subconscious limiting beliefs as they vibrate at such a low frequency. Once you catch them with your conscious mind, and flip them to positive ones, only then your frequency will be aligned and vibrating high. This is when you can manifest with clarity and bring in your ultimate desire into your reality. Recognising this negative vibration becomes crucial. Money, like everything else in the universe, is energy. With humans worldwide focusing their energy on money, it holds an incredibly powerful force. It's been part of human history for thousands of years and has undergone transformations from the bartering system to metallic tokens, to paper, to digital forms. Having positive thoughts about money and being in alignment with those feelings creates positive results. I often guide my clients to imagine money as a person. I tell them to give it a gender and a name. This person, I tell them, will be with you for your entire life, standing right beside you, from birth to passing. This person only follows one simple rule: *whatever energy you give him, he will reflect back to you twofold.* If you give him stress, he will give you double stress back. If you give him worry or lack, he does the same. If you give him love and belief, he will give you double that love back. Therefore, how you regard money directly influences its energy's reflection back to you. Money always gives you something in return. Every interaction involving money is an exchange of energy. When buying something material, or even paying for electricity, gas or food, you always get something in return. Even when receiving a fine, you are getting an exchange. In this instance, you're getting a message to 'slow down', or 'be more focused'.

    Understanding this dynamic and examining our relationship with money can help reprogram negative thoughts and improve our energy exchanges. The key is to realise that the energy we give to money will always bring that vibration in return, so it is important to alter our perspective to a more positive and grateful one. Whenever

I invested positive energy towards money, it reflected that precisely back into my reality. New opportunities emerged, surprising me with the arrival of what I once thought was impossible which resulted in increased financial abundance. It was a flow—as I directed my focus to maintaining positive and grateful thoughts towards everything I purchased, regardless of its monetary value, I sensed a reciprocal surge of positive vibrations in my life. My experiences became more fulfilling as I purposefully cultivated a sense of abundance and eradicated any feelings of lack. In the past, a simple purchase like an eighteen-dollar burger would trigger a negative response, with me exclaiming, 'That's so expensive!' This reaction would taint the entire experience—making the meal less enjoyable or seemingly inadequate. Realising this pattern, I consciously shifted my vibration towards a positive outlook. The next time I was faced with an eighteen-dollar burger, I embraced a different perspective, exclaiming, 'Can't wait to relish this amazing meal. I deserve it.' This shift transformed my experience entirely.

Complaining about money emits a vibration of scarcity, reinforcing a perpetual struggle. Therefore, reflecting back to you exactly that frequency in your reality. To break free from this cycle, immediate changes in thoughts, feelings and vibrations are essential for tangible results. Now that you grasp this concept, start today by tuning in to positive money vibrations. Observe how effortlessly abundance will begin to flow into your life. Embrace these three powerful affirmations:

'I always have more money than I need.'
'It is always easy for me to attract money into my life.'
'I am so happy and grateful now that money comes to me in increasing quantities, through multiple sources on a continuous basis.'

Watch as these affirmations reshape your reality. I persist in reciting these affirmations daily, ensuring my alignment with a positive energy towards money. It never ceases to amaze me how numerous opportunities emerge, enriching my life with more financial abundance. I've reached a point where I no longer harbour negative emotions about deserving the life I envision. Deservingness stands as a major barrier to receiving, yet when one's heart is open to deserving and imagining the life one desires, the realm of possibilities expands. Claim what you want—it's your birthright to shape and manifest your dreams and desires. Your thoughts, feelings and vibration are the sole factors that can hinder or propel you towards this reality. The key to harnessing the power of your consciousness lies in recognising and transforming negative thoughts as they arise, channelling them into positive ones that affirm your self-worth and align with your desires. This process represents the essence of true consciousness, where you are fully present and actively engaged in your thoughts, feelings and vibration. It involves intentionally cultivating *deliberate thinking*, which is a conscious choice aimed at shaping and manifesting the life you desire. You have the power to deliberately create your reality. Make a conscious decision to infuse your thoughts with positivity, love and possibility. By doing so, you activate the magical process of manifesting your dreams into reality. Remember, it all starts with a choice. Choose to be conscious. Choose to be deliberate in your thoughts and feelings. Choose to vibrate high. Choose to respond instead of reacting. You have the power to shape your reality and create the life that resonates with your deepest desires. So, let's take a moment to reflect. Become aware of the thoughts that flow through your mind. Are they in alignment with the life you wish to create? If not, gently guide your focus towards thoughts that uplift, inspire and empower you.

You are the master of your own destiny, and it's time to be a deliberate thinker. As you practise this principle, watch as your reality transforms before your eyes. The Universe eagerly awaits your conscious choice to create a life filled with joy, abundance and limitless possibilities. You first have to believe in yourself, step into your power and let deliberate thinking become the guiding force that shapes your reality. You have the ability to craft a life that reflects your true essence and brings you immense fulfilment. Choose wisely and consciously as you enjoy the magic on the remarkable adventure of deliberate creation. It's time for you to become vigilant, to pay attention to where you reside in your consciousness. This journey begins with self-responsibility and the power of questioning.

EXERCISE
What am I thinking?

Use these blank pages to write down your daily thoughts. Start by listing what you thought today. Feel free to add to it in the following days to come.

_____

_____

_____

_____

_____

_____

_____

_____

_____

_____

_____

_____

_____

_____

_____

Take a moment to reflect on these thoughts and feelings that shape your perception of life.
- Are they serving you?
- Do they align with the life you desire?
- Do they align with your 'desired state of life' pie chart?
- How many thoughts are negative?
- How many thoughts are on repeat?

You now have the awareness to eliminate the thoughts that no longer serve you and begin creating new thoughts that do.

This practice of continual questioning is the gateway to self-improvement. It helps us break free from the confines of victimhood and step into our innate strength. As we consciously choose how we think, feel and vibrate, we reclaim our power and shape our own reality. We become deliberate creators.

Now, let's embrace the power of positive thoughts and creating alignment. Incorporate them into your daily practice, for they hold immense transformative strength. With each affirming word you speak, think and feel, you begin the shift towards a new state of being and a new reality. It's time to reposition yourself from a place of limitation to a place of empowerment. Adopt the practice of speaking words that uplift, feel inspired, happy and at peace and align with the vibration to bring in the life you desire. Let these positive thoughts and feelings become a mantra that resonates within you. Remember to fully feel like you are in the place of being and having these things already.

By consciously infusing our days with positive thoughts and feelings, we lay the foundation for a significant shift in our state of being. We unlock the door to a new reality—one filled with joy, abundance and limitless possibilities.

Trust in your ability to shape your own destiny. Let positivity become your daily companion, guiding you towards a state of empowerment and fulfilment. Believe in the power of your mind, for it has the potential to create a profound shift in your life. Embrace this practice with love and determination and watch as your reality blossoms into a beautiful reflection of your inner strength and joy.

Remember, all in all the Universe operates on a remarkable principle: it reflects back to us the energy we send out. If we perceive ourselves as a victim, the Universe will present us with countless opportunities that reinforce this belief. This is where the Law of Attraction comes into play. It's a universal law that states what we think about and focus on is what we attract into our lives. Our thoughts and intentions shape the reality we experience. Sadly, too often, our subconscious thoughts lean towards negativity. As a result, our days become a rollercoaster ride, filled with ups and downs, rather than the smooth flowing river we desire. We find ourselves saying things like, 'I hate traffic. I hate waiting. I always attract rude people.' Here's the key: these thoughts and feelings create a predominant state within us. They carry a specific frequency that resonates with the experiences we continuously attract.

Now, take a moment to reflect on this profound truth. Understand that you hold the power to shift your predominant state. You can transform the frequency you send out into one that aligns with the life you truly desire. As you choose to focus on positive thoughts and intentions, you automatically replace the habit of dwelling on what you dislike and shift your attention towards what brings you joy, freedom and abundance. As you consciously choose to align your thoughts and energy with positivity, you'll witness a remarkable transformation in your life. The Universe, in its infinite wisdom, then responds by bringing forth experiences, people and opportunities that resonate with your newfound state of being.

Remember, you are the co-creator of your own existence. By consciously shifting your predominant state, you open the door to a world of endless possibilities. Open your heart and watch as the Universe mirrors your positive vibration, manifesting a reality that reflects your true essence and desires. You hold the key. Embrace the power of your thoughts, feelings, intentions and energy. Let them be a magnet for all that you wish to attract. Trust in the process, believe in your ability to shape your own reality and witness the magic unfold before your eyes. It all starts with becoming aware of your thoughts. This simple practice requires you to be present, to embrace moments of quiet contemplation without judgment. When you sense discord, disharmony or suffering, resist the urge to immediately fix or control the situation. Instead, find a serene space and sit quietly. Take a deep breath and dive into self-reflection. Ask yourself:

- What am I feeling?
- What is unfolding within me?
- What thoughts and emotions am I creating?
- Most importantly, what lesson lies within this experience?

Through these introspective inquiries, you unveil the hidden treasures that reside within every moment. Even amidst challenges, there are valuable lessons to be learnt and opportunities for growth and transformation.

In this sacred space of self-reflection, you'll discover insights that guide you towards a life of authenticity and fulfilment. Embrace the gifts that await you and let them propel you forwards on the path of self-realisation and joyful living. Your awareness holds tremendous power. It serves you in two profound ways that lead to growth and transformation. Be present in each passing moment and gently explore the depths of your thoughts and feelings. As you do so, you open the door to self-discovery and a deeper understanding of yourself and the world around you. Within every experience, there is a gift waiting to be recognised. It may be a lesson, a chance for personal growth or a shift in perspective. By acknowledging and embracing these gifts, we unlock the potential for deep transformation and a life enriched with purpose and meaning.

First, by acknowledging your feelings, you honour their existence. Your emotions are real and valid, and they should never be negated or ignored. Accept them with compassion and understanding, for they provide valuable guidance on your journey. Second, through this awareness, you gain precious insights into your creations and the gifts hidden within challenges. Every experience, even the most difficult ones, holds within it an opportunity for growth and change. By recognising the lessons and blessings that come with each challenge, you unlock the door to personal evolution. As you courageously acknowledge your feelings and delve deeper into the insights they bring, you progress on your journey of self-discovery. By nurturing your awareness, you open the door to a world of endless possibilities that transform your life in ways you never thought possible. Remember, you are a magnificent being capable of incredible growth and change. By recognising the power of your awareness and honouring your feelings, you seek the wisdom hidden within each challenge. You must trust in the process and watch as you unfold into the best version of yourself.

It is a beautiful dance of growth and change, with so many gifts that lie within your awareness. Your thoughts and feelings are the catalysts that inspire you to reach new heights and create a life that resonates with your truest desires. You become aware of your thoughts and gain the ability to redirect them. In these moments of awareness, you hold the key to transform your future experiences. You have the power to replace negative thoughts with affirming words that will shape a brighter reality. Here's the beautiful part: you don't have to dive into healing the negative thoughts themselves. It's not about dwelling on the past or dissecting every limiting belief. All that's required is your awareness and willingness to shift from negative to positive. With each thought you consciously redirect, you sow the seeds of a more joyful and fulfilling future. You begin to program your mind to acknowledging the negative thoughts and actively choosing to replace them with empowering and uplifting ones. Once you have formed this as a daily practice, you will find yourself doing this almost immediately.

You have within you the ability to create a reality that aligns with your deepest desires. By harnessing the power of your awareness and intentionally shifting from negative to positive, you open the door to a world of limitless possibilities. So, now it's time to catch those negative thoughts as they arise. Don't let them define your reality. Instead, choose to immediately insert positive words that reflect the future you wish to experience. Think them, feel them, celebrate them like they have already happened. Allow this transformative energy to flow through your awareness and watch as your life unfolds in ways that surpass your wildest dreams. When you become aware of your thoughts and feelings and imagine your desired outcome as if it's already happened, that's a powerful practice. But if it doesn't yield the results you want, it's time to delve into your subconscious mind. This is where the last principle we discussed comes into play—reprogramming your childhood wounds.

Imagine you're manifesting a specific job. You truly believe you've got it, you can feel it and you align your thoughts with that vision. But then, you don't get the job. This is where the subconscious mind, rooted in childhood experiences, might be interfering, telling you that you're not good enough. Say you are longing for financial abundance and you embark on a journey of positive thinking, envisioning wealth flowing effortlessly into your life. You take inspired actions, moving towards your financial goals. Yet, if your subconscious still holds onto beliefs rooted in childhood wounds, like 'I'm not deserving', it will steer you towards scarcity rather than abundance. This is why reprogramming childhood wounding is crucial. It goes hand in hand with positive thinking and creating alignment. Your wounded inner child needs to be reprogrammed first. So that you have power over your subconscious thoughts because the more aware of them you are, the easier it is to nurture them, silence them and affirm the opposite.

When you manifest, you'll do so without doubt because you've already addressed your childhood trauma. This is a significant element that many spiritual teachers often overlook, but it's the key to manifesting your desires into reality. To simplify, start by healing childhood trauma and reprogramming your beliefs. Then, visualise your desired outcome as if it's already yours and align with the Universe's vibration as you do this. Always ensure that your subconscious mind believes you can have what you desire and that your childhood wounds are not holding you back, as they can be quite influential. Believe in the power of this simple yet profound practice. Trust that by shifting your thoughts from negative to positive, you are actively shaping your destiny. Embrace the journey with an open heart and a willingness to let go of what no longer serves you. In every circumstance we encounter, there lies an opportunity for growth and transformation. Life, in its infinite wisdom, is always supporting us on our journey.

What we truly need is a change of perception when it comes to our experiences. Instead of seeing life as something that happens *to* us, we can shift our perspective and embrace the belief that life is happening *for* us. When we adopt this empowering viewpoint, we open ourselves up to a world of possibilities. We recognise that every challenge, every setback and every moment of joy is a stepping stone on our path of personal evolution. Life becomes our ally, our teacher and our greatest supporter. We no longer feel like victims of circumstance, but rather co-creators of our own destiny. We understand that every experience serves a purpose, whether it's to teach us a valuable lesson, strengthen our resilience or lead us closer to our dreams. So, I invite you to shift your perspective. Embrace the belief that life is happening for you, shifting to the perception that incredible opportunities await you. Believing that life is happening for you and watch as the Universe aligns with your newfound perspective, paving the way for a life filled with abundance, joy and endless possibilities. Open your heart and mind to the opportunities that present themselves in each moment. As you make this shift in perception, you'll begin to see the beauty and synchronicities that unfold in your life. You'll find strength and inspiration in the face of challenges, knowing that they are catalysts for your personal growth and learning lessons. Trust that every experience, whether pleasant or difficult, is guiding you towards a more fulfilling and purposeful existence. Believe in your ability to create your own reality. Remember, you have the power to see life from a new vantage point. Your journey of growth and transformation starts now.

Among the multitude of teachings and belief systems suggesting various universal laws, these concepts are grounded in metaphysical and spiritual beliefs. Individuals often practise these laws based on what resonates with them. Although there's no unanimously agreed-upon set of laws for manifesting desires, here are some commonly discussed universal laws related to manifestation. These laws hold transformative power and definitely guide you on a journey towards bringing your desired reality to life. One popular book written by

Herbert Harris is *"The Twelve Universal Laws of Success"*. These laws include *The Law of Divine Oneness, the Law of Vibration, the Law of Correspondence, the Law of Attraction, the Law of Inspired Action, the Law of Perpetual Transmutation of Energy, the Law of Cause and Effect, the Law of Compensation, the Law of Relativity, the Law of Polarity, the Law of Rhythm* and *the Law of Gender*.

In my experience and perspective, three laws stand out as the most potent in bringing our desired reality to life. *Law of Attraction, Law of Deliberate Creating* and *Law of Allowing*.

The first is the *Law of Attraction*. It's a fundamental law of the universe that states what we truly want, what we think about and focus on, is what we ultimately bring into our life experience. Our thoughts and intentions have the power to shape our reality.

Next, we have the *Law of Deliberate Creating*. This is about consciously and intentionally creating our lives. It's about taking charge of our days, practicing focus and belief and truly embodying the idea that we already have what we desire. It's about becoming active participants in the creation of our own destiny.

Finally, we have the *Law of Allowing*. This law teaches us the importance of being open and receptive to the abundance and wonders of life. It's about letting events and situations unfold naturally and having gratitude for the blessings we have attracted into our lives. It's about being opened to receive, accept and appreciate all that we create.

By understanding and aligning ourselves with these universal laws, we tap into our power and highest potential. We become deliberate creators of our reality, attracting the experiences and manifestations that align with our deepest desires. Allow the *Law of Attraction* to work in your favour as you focus your thoughts and intentions on what you truly desire. Embrace the *Science of Deliberate Creating* as you consciously create your life with intention and belief. And practise the *Art of Allowing* as you open yourself to receive and appreciate the abundance that surrounds you. Together, these three laws empower us to live a life of purpose, fulfilment and limitless possibilities. Welcome them with an open heart and a willingness to believe in your own creative power. You have the ability to shape your reality and manifest the life of your dreams. Trust in the magic of these universal laws and trust in them as guiding lights on your journey. The Universe is ready to align with your intentions and bring forth all that you desire. You have the power within you, so let the miracles unfold.

What is it that you truly desire? It's the big question. Many of us are well aware of what we *don't* want in life, but when asked about our true desires, we often struggle to picture a life filled with comfort, serenity and boundless freedom. The reason many of us struggle to imagine a life of freedom and abundance is because it's something we've never personally experienced. It's difficult to picture something that feels so far from our reality. Often, we hold on to negative and limiting beliefs that are deeply ingrained in our subconscious and unconscious minds. These beliefs are reinforced by our past experiences and the wounds from our childhood. We tend to believe that the life of our dreams is for someone else, not us. We see people who seem to have it all, with successful and fulfilling lives, and we label them as 'lucky'. It feels like that kind of life is out of reach for us. But this is not the truth. In reality, every one of us has the potential to create a life filled with abundance and happiness. The universe is boundless, and its possibilities are limitless. We have the power to tap into this abundance, but it starts with changing our beliefs and aligning our thoughts and feelings with the life we desire. It's about breaking free from the constraints of our past and realising that we, too, can manifest a life of abundance. Once we've clearly identified our aspirations, it's time to align our vibrations with the Universe. It's about tuning in to the exact frequency that resonates with our desires, enabling us to attract and achieve them. This process begins with knowing what we want, but the true magic lies in our unwavering belief that *we deserve it*.

Expressing gratitude for what we already have serves as a portal to welcoming more of our heart's desires. It opens the floodgates for abundance and allows us to receive the blessings we seek.

Gratefulness is the doorway to receiving.

EXERCISE
Deliberate Creating

Deliberately create the day you desire. Take a moment in the morning to envision everything you want to unfold throughout your day. Be specific in your thoughts and feelings, connect energetically to each aspect you desire to appear in your day, allow yourself to immerse in the experience as if it has already come to fruition.

Every morning, start your day by writing down what you want to create on that day. This could be anything you desire and it's not limited to physical things—it includes your feelings, events and interactions with people. The key is to immerse yourself in these desires and feel as if they have already happened. For example, you might write, 'I feel at peace', 'I excel at work', 'I have amazing conversations', 'I connect with my family.' or perhaps, 'I receive an invitation that makes me happy.' or more general desires like, 'I receive good news today', 'I receive a gift.' or 'I attract a nice surprise.' The entire process is about manifesting these desires, embracing the feelings of already having them and being opened to receiving them. Gratitude plays a significant role here.

Every night, review your list and check off the desires that came true. For the ones that didn't, explore your subconscious mind. Sometimes, limiting beliefs might be holding you back, or certain desires may need more time. Trust in divine timing and feel free to set the same intentions for the next day. This practice helps you take control of your life and attract the things you want. Conclude by taking a moment to thank the Universe for the wonderful things that occurred. Be grateful every night.

You possess the power to mould your day and live the life you desire. By deliberately creating your desires each day, and infusing your thoughts with positive feelings that align with those intentions, you set in motion the process of true manifestation. This is where the magic happens.

As you follow this practice, you'll experience the incredibly rewarding results of watching your desires come to life in your reality.

Have you ever noticed how some people are always focused on the negatives in their life? They seem to constantly talk about their pains, limitations, past hurts and financial struggles, focusing on everything they dislike. It's as if they're stuck in a loop of negativity, unable to break free. They constantly talk about their struggles, as if life will never improve and they're destined to suffer. It's like they find comfort in playing the victim, believing that these unfortunate circumstances are all they'll ever have. But what if I told you that they have the power to change their reality?

Here's the thing: every moment of pain they experience has been created by their own thoughts, feelings and vibrations. Dwelling on what they *don't* want only amplifies more of its presence in their lives. It keeps them trapped in a cycle of discontent and prevents them from embracing the abundance and joy that is available to them. Instead, they need to shift their perspective by focusing on the good, the possibilities and the things they love. By shifting their attention to what brings them happiness, they can start to attract more of it. They rise their vibration and begin to manifest from there. The good news is they have the ability to transform their pain into their power.

It's about consciously choosing to see the beauty in our lives, even amidst challenges. Rather than complaining and talking about our struggles, we must shift our conversations towards our dreams, ideas, aspirations and the things that ignite our passion. By surrounding ourselves with positive thoughts, positive people and affirmations, we empower ourselves to create the life we truly desire. Remember, we have the power to shape our reality through our thoughts and emotions. So, we must begin to choose to uplift ourselves. By shifting our focus to the positive aspects of life, we open ourselves up to a world of endless possibilities and true fulfilment. Deep within each of us lies the untapped potential to create the life we truly desire. We just need to be willing to put in the work. It takes commitment, discipline, motivation and unwavering focus.

Stay motivated and remember that you have the power to shape your own destiny. With dedication and perseverance, you can break free from the chains of negativity and create a life filled with purpose, joy and abundance. It's an undeniable truth that you possess the incredible power to shape and transform your reality. You hold within you the ability to break free from the constraints that hold you back, whether they are physical, emotional, or mental. Moreover, it's awe-inspiring to consider that your mind and emotions can even contribute to healing and overcoming illness.

What if you switched gears and cultivated a positive mindset? What if you consciously chose to speak, think and feel positively, creating a life that aligns with your deepest dreams and aspirations? Can you imagine the possibilities that would unfold? Embracing positivity is a game-changer. It opens up a world of infinite potential and endless opportunities. By shifting your thoughts and feelings towards the positive, you invite a wave of transformation into your life. You become an active participant in shaping your destiny, manifesting your dreams and experiencing a life that goes beyond your wildest imagination. Harnessing the power of positive thinking and letting your thoughts and emotions become the guiding force behind your reality is the greatest give of self-love. Commit yourself to this principle and believe you have the power and inner resources to unleash your true potential.

Imagine waking up each day with a renewed sense of purpose and excitement. Imagine envisioning a life where your dreams are within reach and where happiness and abundance are the norm. It's all possible when you choose to embrace the transformative power of positivity. Start today and watch as the Universe begins to respond to your newfound positive energy. Begin by rewiring your negative thoughts and embracing the power of positivity. It all starts with awareness.

Let's break it down into simple steps:

1. Become aware of negative thoughts
Pay attention to the thoughts that bring you down. Notice when you feel depressed, lack money or are surrounded by negative people. *Awareness* is the key to change.

2. Catch your negative thoughts and flip them to positive thoughts
Once you catch those negative thoughts, it's time to counteract them with positive affirmations. For instance, when you catch yourself thinking, *'I am bored'* affirm with, *'I feel happy.'* When you catch yourself thinking, *'I don't have enough money,'* affirm with, *'I am abundant.'* And when you think you attract selfish people, affirm with, *'I always attract kind and considerate individuals.'*

3. Repeat and reinforce
Affirmations are most effective when repeated consistently. Make it a habit to affirm positive statements daily. Repeat them with conviction and belief. Vibrate to the exact frequency of having it already in your reality. Over time, they will help reprogram your mind and shift your energy towards positivity, changing your cells and reprogramming your subconscious mind.

4. Embrace the transformation
As you continue to replace negative thoughts with positive affirmations, watch how your perspective begins to shift. You'll find yourself naturally attracting more happiness, abundance and kind-hearted individuals into your life.

Remember, this process requires patience and persistence. It may not happen overnight, but every small step counts. Celebrate the progress you make along the way and stay committed to the journey of self-transformation. You hold the power to reprogram your thoughts and manifest a reality that aligns with your most heartfelt desires. Embrace the positive, embrace the change and watch as your life begins to unfold in beautiful and unexpected ways.

As I became aware of my negative thoughts and committed to transforming them into positive ones, remarkable changes began to unfold in my life. It was a daily practice that required consistency and commitment. Initially, I challenged myself to do this for at least thirty days and these days, I do it every day of my life. Shifting from negative to positive thoughts was difficult at first, as I had ingrained these negative thought patterns for so long. They played on repeat, almost like a habit. But my determination to change kept me going. Over time, I put my focus and belief into this principle, driven by the desire for personal growth and transformation. And I can tell you, over time, it became second nature. When a negative thought surfaced, it felt like a fire burning within my stomach and I could easily identify it in my body. Consequently, I learnt to flip it immediately into a positive thought. Within seconds, I could clear my mind of negativity and limiting beliefs, replacing them with positive ones.

This practice became fun, like a daily game, watching the results and manifestations coming into my reality. I've dedicated myself to this technique for years, making it a daily ritual. This journey of self-discovery and growth is ongoing. As long as we're human beings, we continue to evolve and learn, and I find that process exciting. The more I commit to my spiritual growth and persist in replacing negative patterns with positive ones, the more I witness the magic unfold. The Universe, in all its wisdom, starts aligning with my new vibration. My mind, body and soul resonate with positive energy and as a result, the Universe orchestrates changes in my life to manifest my dreams effortlessly. I know I'm doing the work correctly because these changes become evident in my physical reality. Opportunities present themselves with ease, like-minded people are drawn to me, and I attract deep, inspiring conversations. The Universe conspires in my favour. I'm continually amazed by the power I have within me to shape my own reality. By catching and flipping my thoughts, I open the door to unlimited possibilities. I am no longer bound by the limitations of the past or the negative beliefs that once held me back.

The Universe is like my best friend, helping bring my dreams into reality, like a magical magnet attracting my desires into my daily life. I also understand the divine timing of bigger manifestations, never letting go of them until they materialise, embracing patience and trusting the unfolding of the process and knowing the Universe will bring them into my reality in due time. I wholeheartedly believe in the enchantment of life and that we are in control of our own reality. There are days when I'm not entirely sure what I want and during those moments, I simply ask for peace and happiness, allowing beautiful surprises to unfold naturally. My trust in the Universe is unwavering and my foremost belief is that, *'everything works out for me.'*

Commit to consistently shifting your thoughts and watch as the Universe responds in magnificent ways. Your dreams are within reach, and you have the power to bring them to life. Trust the process, believe in yourself and witness the miracles that unfold along the way.

The work we do to understand our past is all about gaining self-awareness and charting a new course for ourselves. It's crucial that we don't dwell on the past reality, as doing so only perpetuates the same experiences we've had before. As we journey forwards with our newfound discipline, it's quite natural to face tests along the way. Elevating ourselves often involves challenges that serve as a way of ensuring we've truly learnt our lessons.

In these moments, you may encounter situations that trigger old negative beliefs you once held. This is a pivotal part of the process, allowing you to recognise what you used to do and how you responded in the past. By observing these tests, you can see that your old ways are no longer necessary or acceptable in the new reality you're manifesting. These tests serve as opportunities for you to identify and transform them, aligning with the new positive vibration you desire. It's all part of the beautiful journey of growth and transformation.

Our manifestations take time to unfold within the space-time continuum of our lives. We must keep this in mind and resist getting caught up in old cycles that may still be playing out. Instead, our focus should be on what we're creating in each present moment. We need to shift our mindset away from the past, which is familiar but limiting and start living in the feeling of the person we aspire to be. This is where we are actively creating our *'future self'*.

Let's now focus on the person you want to become, rather than the person you used to be. With each moment, you have the opportunity to shape your reality and manifest your dreams. It's a continuous journey of growth, but by consciously choosing to create a new direction, you unlock the potential for a brighter future. Believe in the power you possess to redefine your life. Embrace the present and let go of the past. With determination, self-awareness and a vision of the person you aspire to become, you can create a future filled with endless possibilities. It's time to step into your own greatness and live the life you've always imagined.

Now, it's time to envision and create your *future self*—the person you truly desire to be. It's about manifesting the life you want to live, the emotions you want to feel, the experiences you crave and the state of being that brings you joy. And the key lies in embracing the feeling of already embodying this life. As you align your energy with the vibration that matches your desired future, something magical happens. The gap between your present self and future self begins to narrow. In fact, you are actively creating that future right now. The Universe doesn't know time—there's no different between past, present, or future. All it knows is vibration. When you start aligning yourself with the vibration you want for your future, the Universe fast-tracks the process and hands you those good things right here and now. Your job is to stay aligned to the vibration of those things you want, to feel as though you already are that person, living those feelings of already having the things you desire. The Universe will then do its part. When your vibration—the feeling state you embody—aligns with who you aspire to be, you start seeing evidence of this in your life.

These signs of change may start small, like building blocks that slowly restructure your life. It's important to focus on these positive signs of transformation rather than solely fixating on what is yet to arrive. Stay grounded in the feeling of already having and being what you desire. Remember, change is incremental. By embracing the feeling of already having the life you envision, you attract more of those experiences and opportunities. It's a continuous process of growth and manifestation. So, let go of any doubt or disbelief. Feel the joy, excitement and gratitude of already living the life you desire. With every step you take, every decision you make, you are aligning yourself with that future self. Keep the vision alive within you and trust that the Universe is working in your favour. Your dreams are within reach and by staying aligned with the feeling of already having them, you are paving the way for their manifestation. Stay focused on the positive shifts happening in your life and let your future self-guide your present actions. You are the creator of your own reality and the life you desire is waiting for you to claim it. Let's take a moment to reflect on these empowering questions in preparation for your next exercise. Ask yourself:

1. How do I look?
Visualise yourself in your desired future state. How do you appear? Radiant, confident, healthy and filled with vitality? Imagine the details of the appearance of your transformed self.

2. How do I feel?
Dive into the emotions of your future self. How does it feel to be in that state of being? Do you feel joyful, peaceful, confident and fulfilled? Embrace the positive emotions that come with embodying your desired future.

3. How does it feel to be me?
Connect with the essence of your future self. How does it feel to fully step into your authentic self? Embrace the confidence, purpose and self-assurance that comes with living your truth.

4. What are my new characteristics?
Envision the qualities and traits that define your future self. Are you resilient, compassionate or perhaps adventurous? Embrace the empowering characteristics that align with your desired future.

5. How do I interact with my world?

Imagine the way you engage with the world around you in your desired future. Are you kind, assertive or supportive? Picture yourself creating positive interactions and leaving a meaningful impact on others.

6. What are my primary relationships like?

Visualise the relationships that thrive in your future. Are they filled with love, trust and mutual growth? Imagine harmonious connections and nurturing bonds with the people who matter most to you.

7. How am I contributing to the world?

Consider the ways you contribute to the greater good in your desired future. Are you making a difference through your work, passions, or acts of kindness? Envision yourself living in your purpose, leaving a positive imprint on the world.

8. Where do I live?

Picture your ideal living environment. Is it a cosy home in the countryside, by the beachfront or a vibrant city apartment? Visualise the place that resonates with your future self and brings you a sense of comfort and happiness.

9. What do I experience?

Envision the experiences that enrich your life in your desired future. Do you travel, learn new skills, or embrace adventure? Immerse yourself in the exciting and fulfilling experiences that align with your vision.

10. How do I interact with my world?

See yourself engaging with the world around you in your desired future. Are you open-minded, curious and ready to explore? Embrace a mindset of growth, learning and positive engagement.

Use these questions as an opportunity to help you shape your vision of your future self. Embrace the power of your imagination and let it guide you towards the life you truly desire. With clarity and intention, you can manifest a future that truly aligns with your dreams.

EXERCISE
Create your Future Self

Let's dive into an empowering exercise to craft your future self. Take a moment to connect with your innermost desires, envisioning the person you want to become and the extraordinary life you wish to lead. Consider all the aspects we've discussed earlier. Imagine the best version of yourself, living a life in perfect harmony with your deepest desires. Visualise a future filled with excitement and joy. Ensure you cover every aspect of the life you envision for your future.

Feel free to express this exercise with creativity—whether through writing, drawing, or using arrows around the human outline figure.

Bring your *future self* to your reality
Having crafted the blueprint of your future self and the dream life you aspire to live, it's time to transcend visualisation and immerse yourself in having this reality in the present moment. Consciously embrace the feelings of joy, gratitude and excitement as if you are already living this reality. Trust in the inherent power within you to manifest this envisioned life. As you intensify your focus and genuinely feel like your future self is happening in the present, the gap between the future and the now becomes narrower. Manifestations thrive on the synergy of thoughts and feelings, unwavering belief and the unwavering certainty of possibility.

Be consistent to this practice daily, actively shaping your destiny by embodying the feelings of your future self. Witness the transformative power as opportunities and the emotions associated with your vision manifest in your present reality. Understand that the future you envision is within reach. Keep the flame of your vision alive and behold as your reality undergoes magnificent transformations. Every day, I am fuelled by focused energy towards my future self. Think of it as having a blueprint for a brand-new home. I don't have to worry about the nitty-gritty of construction or figuring out every little detail. Do not think of *how it's going to happen,* just focus on the feeling of *it's already happened.* Instead, I am the one instructing the architect on how it should look and feel. The 'Great Architect of the Universe' will take care of the rest, finding the perfect way to make it all come together. All I need to do is immerse myself in the feeling and knowing that I am already living in this magnificent home. I hold the vision in my heart and mind, believing with unwavering faith that it is my reality. It's about trusting the process and surrendering to the greater forces at work.

Your *physical mind* (human self) is in control of one thing, visualising and feeling you desired reality. Your higher mind (higher self) is in charge of collecting all the details, information and bringing you the outcome that aligns with your desires. With this deep knowing, you are an active participant in co-creating your future. You are shaping the reality you desire by aligning your thoughts, emotions and actions with your vision. Every day, take inspired steps and make choices that align with the life you are building. Sure, there might be challenges along the way, but make sure you embrace them as opportunities for growth and learning. Remain committed to your vision and trust that the Universe is working with you, guiding you towards the manifestation of your dreams. Remember, you have the power within you to create the reality you desire. Trust in yourself and the process. Keep envisioning, believing and taking steps towards your dream. Your future is waiting to unfold, and you are the one who can make it real.

A deliberate thinker is an accurate thinker. They are someone who is fully focused on what they want to manifest in their life, and someone who is in control of their thoughts and emotions. They understand that distractions and resistance may arise, but that they have the power to pull back their attention and realign with their desired reality in the present moment.

Now it's time for you to embrace the mindset of an accurate thinker, knowing that what you desire is already within you. Become grateful for the blessings and manifestations that have already come into your life and grateful for ones that are coming. Live in the energy of abundance and fulfilment, knowing that you are the co-creator of your own experiences. Do not rely on luck or the hand of fate to bring about your desires. Understand that you are constantly creating and manifesting based on what you honestly believe about yourself and the world around you. With this heightened awareness, choose to cultivate positive beliefs and thoughts that support your highest aspirations. Take responsibility for your creations and embrace the power you have to shape your reality. Release any limitations or self-doubt and step into the knowing that you are capable of achieving your dreams. Through intentional thoughts, actions and alignment with your desires, you are actively co-creating the life you envision.

Trust in the process of manifestation and stay committed to your vision. Remain open to the signs and guidance that the Universe provides along the way. With each deliberate thought and focused intention, you are drawing your desires closer to you and bringing them into fruition. Remember, as a deliberate thinker, you have the power to shape your reality. Trust in your own creative abilities and align your thoughts and actions with your deepest desires. Your manifestations are a reflection of what you believe to be true, so choose empowering beliefs and create the life you truly deserve. In the awe-inspiring journey of manifesting your desires, there is a profound truth that sets you apart—the power of gratitude and living in the energy of your manifestations. Imagine already basking in the glorious fulfilment of your dreams, feeling the exhilaration pulsating through your veins.

In this grand cosmic dance, your manifestations emerge as living testaments to your inner landscape. You manifest abundance when you embrace a mindset of abundance. You attract love and harmony when you radiate love and harmony from within. The world bows to your command, mirroring your beliefs and perceptions. No longer shall you be a passive victim of circumstance, but instead, a fierce creator who seizes the reins of your existence. With resolute determination, you need to remove all doubt and limitation. Your creations become the embodiment of your truth, breathing life into the very essence of who you truly are.

As you continue on the path of positive thinking and alignment, remember this sacred truth—your desires are not mere whims; they are your birthright. Express gratitude for what has already come into your life and let that gratitude propel you towards even greater heights. With every heartbeat, every thought and every step, believe wholeheartedly in the power you possess to shape your reality. Let this knowledge ignite a blazing fire within you, fuelling your every endeavour. For you are the master alchemist, transforming your dreams into tangible manifestations. Hold tight to the unshakable knowledge that you hold the key to unlock a world of limitless possibilities.

Welcome to your new reality!

In the dance of light and darkness within, we find the harmony of our wholeness, accepting the depths of our being.

PRINCIPLE

4

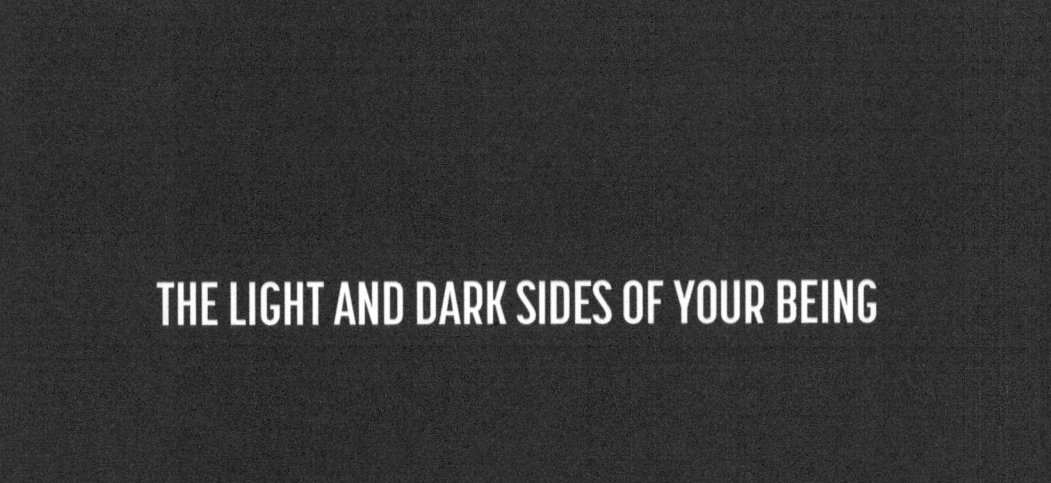

Duality refers to the concept of two opposing or contrasting aspects coexisting together. It is often used to describe situations where there are two sides to something, like heads or tails, up and down, left and right, forwards and back, positive and negative, inside and outside, good and evil and so on. These dualities highlight the balance and complexity within our world and experiences. Duality is a fundamental aspect of many philosophical, spiritual and scientific theories, highlighting the balance and interconnectedness of opposing forces in the universe. Think about it like this: in life, we often encounter things that have contrasting aspects. These dualities are like puzzle pieces that fit together to form a complete picture. They help us understand and appreciate the world around us. So, instead of seeing dualities as separate or conflicting, we can view them as complementary parts that come together to create a whole. They exist side by side, each contributing its own unique qualities, and together they form a balanced and complete experience of life.

Imagine you're in a room with a light switch. When you turn the switch on, the room becomes bright with light. But what happens when you turn the switch off? The room becomes dark. In this example, light represents one aspect or duality, and darkness represents its opposite. Now think about life. Just like this room, life also has different aspects or dualities. Happiness and sadness, success and failure, and other contrasts like these, represent the spectrum of life's experiences. What I've come to understand is that these dualities are not separate entities.

Rather, they coexist, forming an integral part of the whole. Just as light and darkness coexist within the same room, life requires these dualities to be complete.

Think of it as a puzzle. Let's say these pieces represent duality. When you put all the pieces together, you get the full picture, the complete experience of life. Light and dark, and all the other dualities, come together to form this whole picture. Have you ever seen the yin and yang symbol? It's a circle with two parts: one is black (yin) with a small dot of white, and the other is white (yang) with a small dot of black. This symbol represents the idea of duality. It shows that even in darkness (yin), there is a bit of light and in light (yang), there is a bit of darkness. The yin part represents things like earth, femininity, darkness and being calm and receptive. It's like when you're in a quiet, peaceful state. The yang part represents things like heaven, masculinity, light and being active and assertive. Yin and yang represent exactly this concept of duality and how they complement and balance each other out. Together, they symbolise harmony and the dynamic equilibrium found in nature and the universe.

When I was studying for my Masters in Reiki, we explored the meaning of light and dark and why it is important to embrace both sides equally. Learning to accept and understand both sides of our light and dark aspects is crucial for our growth, as they both play significant roles in shaping our life. The word 'guru' actually reflects this idea. The word is made up of two parts: *'gu'* means darkness and *'ru'* means light. A guru is someone who is a spiritual teacher, a mentor or an expert in a certain field. But what makes them special is that they accept both the light and the dark within themselves. They understand the importance of embracing both sides. The yin and yang symbol and the concept of light and dark teach us that duality is a natural part of life, coming together to form a whole. It is important for you to accept and embrace both the light and the dark within yourself. This allows you to have a deeper understanding of your true nature and the world around you.

Have you ever heard of 'shadow work'? It is about exploring the hidden parts of yourself that you may not even realise exist. These hidden parts are stored in your subconscious and unconscious mind, which, as you now know, is like a deep, hidden vault storing your thoughts and feelings. When I refer to shadow work, I am talking about uncovering these hidden parts, shining a light on them and bringing them into your awareness. This can include aspects of your personality that you might not like or you consider undesirable. The purpose of shadow work is to become aware of these hidden aspects and to heal and integrate them. It's bringing the dark, all the hidden parts of yourself, into the light. By doing this, you can further expand in your awareness and consciousness.

The development of our shadow self begins when we are young. As children, we are often told that certain behaviours are not acceptable or loveable. These messages can make us hide or repress parts of ourselves, which then become part of our shadow. Many psychoanalysts, who are experts in understanding the mind, help and support people in recognising these hidden parts of themselves. By identifying these parts, people can connect with their wounds and understand their hidden motivations. Sometimes, with parts of ourselves that we dislike or consider undesirable, we try to hide them and not show them to others. These parts are often called our 'shadow side'. But here's the thing: these shadow parts are actually important for us to feel whole and integrated as individuals. They actually serve us.

The work we're doing here involves bringing these hidden parts into the light, understanding them and accepting them as a part of who we are. It's time to go deeper and rise higher, unlocking even greater personal empowerment.

It's not about holding onto past traumas or negative experiences, but rather about achieving personal freedom by facing and exploring the darker aspects of ourselves, and in turn, loving and embracing them. It's important to recognise that both our dark and light sides are valuable. They are both necessary for us to live authentically and love ourselves completely. We're not trying to turn our dark side into light or ignore it completely. Instead, we want to give these parts of ourselves a voice and allow them to reveal their truth.

As adults, we can establish a new understanding of life by embracing both sides of our nature: the conscious (what we are aware of) and the subconscious (what lies beneath the surface). By doing so, we can learn how these different aspects of ourselves either serve us or hinder us in living authentically. So, the work we're doing is about recognising the parts of ourselves that we may consider undesirable and embracing them as an integral part of who we are. It's not about pushing away our dark side or trying to transform it completely. It's about understanding and integrating all aspects of ourselves to live in our truth and love ourselves completely. It's about loving our dark side and understanding how much it is needed in our life, just as much as our light side.

We often see our 'light' as the good side of us. It's the part of us that we feel proud of and that others admire. But here's the thing: there are times when this 'light' side does not serve us or others well. Isn't it mind blowing? Together we will explore and uncover the invaluable contributions of our dark side, recognising how not only it serves us but also others. It's essential to acknowledge and embrace all aspects of ourselves. Both our light and dark sides are necessary for us to live authentically, to not only survive but also thrive in this world.

In this principle, we will explore and recognise all the parts of your light and dark and we will embrace them both. Only then can you start living in a state of wholeness and truth to yourself. This is what living in your truth really means. Living in your truth means being true to yourself, including being aligned with all aspects of who you are, and knowing when to express yourself in ways that are helpful and serve you and others. When you can achieve this, you'll experience a newfound hope, faith in yourself and a deep gratitude for life, as well as a deep sense of admiration and love for yourself.

It's easy to love the positive, light qualities of yourself, like being generous, empathetic or confident. However, it can be challenging to love the parts of yourself that you might think or have been told are not so desirable, known as your dark qualities, like being upfront, boisterous or controlling. But here's the key: embracing and accepting these parts perceived as less desirable traits of yourself is just as important. They are part of who you are, and they contribute to your unique personality and experiences. By embracing all aspects of yourself, you can cultivate self-love and acceptance on a deeper level. For me, a ground-breaking moment was when I realised how important my 'dark' side was and how much it protected, guided and helped me through so many situations in my life. I was told numerous times in my life these qualities were bad, and I normally felt guilty or shamed when they arose. In our society, we have been conditioned to believe that our darker or less desirable parts are not acceptable. We've been taught that it's inappropriate to speak our truth, to be argumentative or to disagree with others. We've been conditioned to think that in order to feel safe and connected to our social groups, we need to behave in a certain way. This conditioning has led us hiding our perceived dark parts, those aspects of ourselves that we feel may not be accepted by others. As children, we were often told to stay in line or be quiet, even when something was wrong. We learnt that it's important to avoid being seen as difficult or annoying. However, what society failed to teach us is that our feelings, emotions and unique expression are valid and important. They have a purpose and can serve both ourselves and others. Many of us were raised to be people-pleasers and to prioritise being liked by others over expressing ourselves authentically. We were taught not to communicate our true thoughts or feelings unless they were positive or deemed acceptable, to fit in rather than celebrate our uniqueness and differences with others. But here's something to consider: our light side, the side that we usually associate with being good, doesn't always serve us or others, either.

In essence, what I'm saying is that both our dark and light sides have the potential to serve us, or not, in different situations. It's about finding a balance and embracing all aspects of ourselves, whether they are perceived as dark or light. By doing so, we can live more authentically, and in a way that honours our true selves. It's important to recognise that our feelings, emotions and unique expression are valid and have value. It's more complex than the light side being good and the dark side being bad. Both sides have a role to play out, depending on the context. By embracing and integrating all aspects of ourselves, we can live more authentically and honour our true selves.

We'll bring these parts to the forefront and show you just how important they are and how they can serve your highest good. This will allow you to live in your truest self, shining as the person you were meant to be, not influenced by society's ideas, conditioning or programming.

Religion has also played a significant role in creating this split or duality within us. It's the idea of God and the Devil, where being good means being part of God and doing something not so good means being part of the Devil. But here's the thing they didn't tell us: this duality is actually perfect in itself. Good exists because there is bad and bad exists because there is good. They go hand in hand. We can only understand one because we know its opposite. For example, we know what hot feels like because we've experienced cold.

Life has its ups and downs, its peaks and troughs. The only time life becomes a flat line is when we die. Everything in between—the good and the bad, the ups and the downs—is what we call *life*. We're here to experience the full spectrum of duality that life has to offer. It helps us understand who we are and what we truly desire to experience.

My commitment is to guide you to realising that during the good times, embracing happiness and openness is essential. Yet, even in challenging moments, maintaining a sense of gratitude and seeking lessons within the experience is crucial. I don't suggest suppressing your human emotions or denying sadness during tough times. Instead, it's about consciously acknowledging that these challenging moments serve a purpose. They are opportunities for growth and learning.

Life comprises a series of highs and lows and, as we navigate our way through the journey, it allows us to grasp the vital lessons required for personal growth. This process propels us towards our unique mission—to evolve into the best version of ourselves and authentically live in our truth. Indeed, it's about embracing and cherishing both the light and dark qualities within us. Embracing this duality and comprehending its essence is fundamental—it's the very fabric of life itself. We're here to fully experience life, acknowledging that we are spiritual beings enveloped in a human experience. Every feeling and emotion navigated is a pathway towards healing, growth and reaching our highest potential. Ultimately, it's about crafting the life we envision and being the best version of ourselves. Life is an exploration—a journey filled with extraordinary experiences. The shadow or opposing forces in our lives are there for our growth, learning and teachings.

Now you will embrace all the parts of you that you are always trying to hide. By doing so, you can live as your true self and experience personal growth. This duality in life, the ups and downs, helps you understand and appreciate the fullness of life. The opposing forces are essential for your growth and learning, ultimately leading you back to love and your authentic self.

It's time to become whole.

It's important to note that what I'm about to explain doesn't justify acting out, being a bad person or causing harm to others intentionally. Instead, I want to focus on understanding yourself better, developing self-awareness and recognising the interplay between the light and dark sides of your being.

The goal is to live in your truth.

When we talk about embracing the light and dark sides of ourselves, it's not about giving ourselves permission to engage in negative behaviours. It's about gaining a deeper understanding of who we are and the different aspects that make up our identity. By acknowledging both the light and dark within us, we can develop greater self-awareness and recognise the patterns that influence our actions and choices. This awareness empowers us to make conscious decisions aligned with our true selves and values. Consciously choosing when to use each quality depends on the situation. Whilst integrating the light and dark sides of our being, we can navigate challenges with greater clarity and make choices that align with our highest good. This journey of self-discovery and acceptance enables us to live a more fulfilling and empowered life. Living authentically means embracing our whole selves—the parts we consider good and those we perceive as bad. It's about accepting ourselves fully and not hiding or suppressing certain aspects out of fear or societal conditioning.

By honestly completing this next exercise, you can gain insights into both your light and dark sides. Remember, this exercise is not about judging yourself, but rather understanding the different aspects of your personality and examining how they can both serve and challenge you and others.

EXERCISE
Explore the light side of your being

Let's begin by examining your light side using the table over page.

1. Write down the qualities you like about yourself in the left column.
2. In the middle column, write down *how this quality does not serve you.*
3. In the right column, write down *how this quality does not serve others.*

I have provided you with a table from one client as an example.

LIGHT SIDE _Client's Example_

Quality I Like About Myself	How This Quality Does NOT Serve Me?	How This Quality Does NOT Serve Others?
Generous & Giving	People may take advantage of me.	May enable dependancy in others.
Kind & Friendly	I prioritize others' needs over my own	Others may take my kindness for granted.
Energetic	I neglect my own well-being in pursuit of tasks.	Others may expect me to always be energetic.
Determined	I become overly fixated on successs, neglecting work-life balance.	Others may perceive me as rigid and uncompromising.
Confident	I risk overconfidence and don't seek others' input.	Others may see me as arrogant or dismissive.
Open book	I expose my vulnerabilities to those who may use them against me.	Others might not feel comfortable sharing with me.
Truthful	I can encounter conflicts for speaking my mind honestly.	Others might avoid sharing sensitive information with me.
Outgoing & Social	I may overextend myself socially and experience burnout.	Others may expect constant social engagement.
Spiritual Leader	Others may expect constant spiritual guidance and support.	May feel overwhelmed by others' spiritual needs.
Disciplined & Strong-Minded	I may struggle with flexibility and adaptability in certain situations.	Others may find me unyielding and inflexible.

LIGHT SIDE

Quality I Like About Myself	How This Quality Does NOT Serve Me?	How This Quality Does NOT Serve Others?

EXERCISE
Explore the dark side of your being

Now let's shift your focus to your dark side.

1. Write down the qualities you *don't like about yourself* in the left column.
2. In the middle column, write *down how this quality serves you.*
3. In the right column, *write down how this quality serves others.*

I have provided you with a table from one client as an example.

DARK SIDE   Client's Example

Quality I Dislike About Myself	How This Quality Serves Me?	How This Quality Serves Others?
Controlling	Helps me maintain order and structure in my life.	Provides guidance and stability for those around me.
Gossiping	Allows me to bond with others through shared stories and experiences.	Provides a sense of connection and belonging in social groups.
Manipulating	Helps me find creative solutions to complex problems.	Encourages others to consider different perspectives and ideas.
Anxious	Heightens my awareness of potential risks and dangers.	Prompts me to be cautious and vigilant in challenging situations.
Worrier	Keeps me prepared for potential obstacles and uncertainties.	Encourages me to offer support and assistance to alleviate others' worries.
Competitive	Drives me to strive for excellence and push my limits.	Inspires others to improve and excel in their endeavours.
Want to be right	Motivates me to seek knowledge and develop a strong understanding of subjects.	Promotes healthy debate and the pursuit of truth in discussions.
Cutting people off and interrupting them	Keeps conversations concise and efficient.	Encourages more focused and productive interactions for others.
Not compassionate	Encourages me to focus on solutions and take action when needed.	Allows others to develop self-reliance and problem-solving skills.
Judgemental	Pushes me to value critical thinking and intellectual growth.	Encourages others to engage in thoughtful discussions and self-improvement.

DARK SIDE

Quality I Dislike About Myself	How This Quality Serves Me?	How This Quality Serves Others?

Through the powerful exercise, '**Explore the light and dark sides of your being**', what did you realise about yourself?

How ground breaking was that exercise for you? Did you grasp its immense significance? Can you acknowledge the importance of your 'dark side' and how much it serves you and others? Did you realise just how valuable it is—much more than you ever knew? Did you also notice the significance of recognising when your 'light side' may *not* serve you or others?

I'm confident that the realisations and self-discoveries you've just encountered will bring about a significant and powerful shift in your perspective and life journey. Conscious living is all about finding balance between both sides of yourself. It means being aware and in tune with your emotions and inner feelings in every situation and interaction with others. It's essential to accept and embrace both the positive and negative aspects of your nature and the qualities they bring. It's about realising you have the power to choose which quality of yourself is needed in response to various situations in your life, and to be conscious of which quality best serves yourself and your highest good. It's about choosing consciously and deliberately the quality that you feel serves you for the best outcome. Self-control plays a pivotal role here. It's not about controlling others. Rather, it's about being consciously aware of your responses and selecting the aspects of yourself that yield the results you seek. It's about being in control of your emotions and responses, instead of having your emotions been in control of you and reacting. When you experience an emotional response to a situation, it's important to acknowledge that it is valid and should be trusted. If you already understand your underlying wounds or triggers, you can determine whether your reaction is simply a knee-jerk effect or a thoughtful and intentional response.

This awareness allows us to respond from a place of balance, neutrality and clarity. We can consciously choose an aspect of ourselves that best suits the situation or addresses any disturbances in our relationships. When we can do this with control and self-awareness, that's when we truly tap into our personal power. Exercising mindful and deliberate responses enables us to achieve the desired outcomes we seek. True power comes from having a clear understanding of what is happening around us and recognising which part of ourselves needs to be expressed in each situation. We utilise our emotions as guideposts, using them as valuable information rather than reactive weapons. Conscious living involves finding balance between both sides of ourselves. By being aware of our emotions and responding mindfully, we can tap into our personal power and achieve desired outcomes. Clarity and self-awareness allow us to discern the appropriate response in each situation, using our emotions as guideposts rather than reacting impulsively.

Let's say I'm renovating my kitchen and the carpenters initially quoted me 5,000 dollars and promised to complete the project in one week. However, after four weeks, they still haven't finished and now they want to charge me double the price. When I find myself in such a situation, I experience emotions such as anger, frustration, betrayal and disappointment. It's important to acknowledge that these emotions are valid and are trying to communicate something to me. They are prompting me to take action so that I can feel happy, satisfied and content with the situation. On the other hand, there might be a part of me, the 'trauma self', that tells me my feelings are not important and that things never work out in my favour. This may push me to respond from my light side to keep myself safe and avoid conflict. It might also encourage me to stay silent and be nice and polite. This, however, is not serving my highest good. Finding the balancing point means recognising that I can also draw upon my dark side, which includes qualities like assertiveness, control and firmness. By embracing these qualities, I can effectively communicate my expectations and needs to the carpenters. This assertive approach serves both me and the carpenters by ensuring that the job is completed as initially agreed upon.

In summary, when faced with a situation like the kitchen renovation example, it's important to acknowledge and honour our emotions as they guide us towards taking appropriate action. While the light side might encourage us to prioritise harmony, finding the balancing point involves utilising qualities from our dark side, such as assertiveness, to reiterate our needs clearly and achieve the desired outcome.

In essence, it's crucial to recognise the significance of embracing both your light and your dark side, fostering self-awareness to unite them into a harmonious whole. This unity allows you to access your personal power. Both aspects are integral in living in your truth, serving not only yourself but also the world around you. Embrace the wonder of your being and the duality inherent in truthful living, and how it aligns with the essence of your soul. Moving forwards, aim to operate from a place of calm and balance. Consciously choose which side and which quality of yourself best suits various situations, utilising it purposefully. Then return to your centre, embracing tranquillity. It's within this tranquil state that you'll truly grasp the essence of inner peace. Understanding both the light and dark sides of your being allows you to acknowledge and integrate all aspects of yourself. It is all about the nurturing of the light while acknowledging and understanding when to harness the power of the dark. This is the essence of wholeness and true self love.

As you find yourself midway through this transformative formula, it's time to cultivate an abundance of self-love, allowing it to deepen and expand within you. With each principle, your love for yourself deepens and fosters an overflow of love for others, as your capacity to love others mirrors the love you hold for yourself. Ultimately, this journey is about self-love, which is the pinnacle of human experience. It marks the initiation of a profound love affair with yourself, embracing both the light and dark sides, living authentically and embracing every facet of your being with unapologetic beauty.

Enjoy the full spectrum of the light and dark sides of your being. Welcome to your wholeness!

Finding love within ourselves stems from embracing the balance of our feminine and masculine energies, echoing the connections in the world around us.

PRINCIPLE 5

FEMININE AND MASCULINE POWER

Welcome to the next principle, where an even deeper expansion of self-love awaits. You will now undertake a journey to unite with the most significant relationship of all, the one with yourself. Before delving deeper, let's take a moment to examine the energies and powers that constitute this relationship. In this universe, there are two fundamental forces that exist in equal measure: the divine feminine and the divine masculine. These powers can be likened to the complementary energies of Mother Earth and Father Sky, or the embodiments of God and Goddess. As human beings, we all embody both of these energies within us. This has nothing to do with gender, nor do they have anything to do with sexuality. Males and females can tap into both energies but will generally operate from one dominant power.

Take a minute to reflect on which core energy you naturally resonate with and acknowledge which one feels most natural to you. In a society filled with blurred lines between masculine and feminine roles, there's a prevalent push for women to adopt more masculine traits for success and survival. However, this can lead to issues because real power emanates from embracing feminine energy. True feminine power stems from a place of deep self-awareness, breaking free from societal pressures and expectations. While masculine power is beneficial in security and action, it's vital to remain connected to both powers.

Think of a male friend who freely shares his emotions without hesitation, drawing from his feminine energy, or a female friend with a determined, go-getter attitude, drawing from her masculine energy. This shows that both men and women can predominantly exhibit either feminine or masculine energies. Living a balanced life entails bridging and integrating these inherent polarities. It is essential for these powers/energies to work harmoniously together in order to discover our unique path and find true balance within. To achieve this, it is important to respect, appreciate, honour and listen to the guidance and gifts of these energies within ourselves. This creates a state of balance and enables us to establish healthy relationships, firstly with ourselves and therefore causing a ripple effect with those around us.

Feminine power represents qualities such as flowing, free, open, emotion-driven, nurturing, creativity, fertility, compassion and warmth. It manifests in stillness, as it is in moments of quiet that we become receptive, innovative and healed. It wants to gather, create, talk and vent. It desires trust, connection and praise. Feminine power is deeply connected to our emotions and inner landscape. It is through our feminine nature that we tap into our great power, including intuition, purpose, creativity and the realm of endless possibilities. Feminine energy is unpredictability. It operates outside the confines of logic and societal norms. It is only guided by the heart's intuition, constantly evolving and adapting. Feminine power comes from embracing one's inner self and facing both light and dark. This energy isn't afraid of confronting inner struggles because it's where true power lies. It sees possibilities beyond what logic dictates, allowing for the creation of new opportunities. Feminine energy manifests effortlessly. It aligns with the frequency of desired experiences and effortlessly draws them in like a magnet. When individuals tap into their feminine energy, they connect with intuition and receive guidance from within. Expression and creation are essential for feminine energy, as it thrives on these aspects. Recognising when to let go of the old to make space for the new is also crucial. It understands the importance of slowing down to nurture oneself, following the natural rhythms of life and renewal. Instead of suppressing emotions, feminine energy embraces them as valuable messengers, listening and learning from their lessons. It dives deep into the soul, emerging stronger. The focus isn't just on reaching a destination but finding creative paths, even ones not on the map, by bending time and space if necessary.

On the other hand, **masculine power** represents qualities such as strength, logic, security, directness, resilience, predictability and is purpose-driven. It is goal-oriented, functional and remains clear and focused. It wants to problem-solve, loves a challenge and is competitive. This energy is like a builder, responsible for taking action and constructing the necessary foundations that provide safety and security. Masculine energy brings stability, willpower and focus. It needs admiration and appreciation. It thrives on creating structures and following logical rules. With its clarity, masculine energy knows what needs to be done and isn't clouded by confusion. It's protective and can detect danger, fighting for what it loves and staying true to its principles, even if it means facing challenges. It values truth and honesty over popularity and wants to be respected and needed. Masculine energy loves doing what's right, regardless of personal sacrifice. It is about shaping destiny and fulfilling life's purpose. This power sometimes needs to make tough decisions, leaving behind what no longer serves. The masculine energy follows a plan but isn't afraid to adjust it to align with its values.

Both feminine and masculine energies exist within each of us, and we draw upon them as needed. To effectively utilise both aspects of ourselves, it is crucial to establish a healthy relationship between our inner feminine and inner masculine powers. The feminine has the inspired ideas; the masculine brings them to fruition. By nurturing a balanced interplay between these powers, we harness their combined strength to achieve a harmonious integration of our desires, visions and actions. In our bodies, the feminine energy resides on the left side of our body, while the masculine energy resides on the right side. The feminine energy represents our receptive nature, where we tap into our creativity and desires. The masculine energy represents our active side, where we express ourselves, take action and deliver results.

In simple terms, it's like this: she asks, and he delivers. She dreams, and he brings those dreams to life. She shows him affection, and he gives her his undivided attention. She offers comfort, and he protects. She expresses gratitude towards him, and he values her deeply. She respects him, and he listens attentively. She appreciates him, and he admires her. This beautiful dance between the feminine and masculine energies is a harmonious exchange of giving and receiving, nurturing and providing, respecting and listening and ultimately, loving and being loved unconditionally. Let's go deeper and rise higher whilst we investigate some thought-provoking questions about the balance of feminine and masculine energies within you, as well as the dynamics of your relationship with yourself:

1. Are you in balance with your feminine and masculine energies?
Do you feel a harmonious interplay between your receptive, creative and nurturing aspects (feminine) and your active, expressive and providing qualities (masculine)?

2. Reflect on your relationship with yourself
How do you treat and nurture yourself? Do you honour and appreciate all aspects of who you are? Are you receptive to your own desires and dreams? Are you taking action to manifest those dreams and express your authentic self?

3. In your partnership with yourself: what is she asking for and is he providing it for her?
Are her needs, desires and dreams being heard, understood and fulfilled? Is there a mutual exchange of affection, attention and respect? Is he actively engaged in creating a safe and supportive space for her to flourish?

4. Consider their feelings towards each other
Does she appreciate and respect him? Does he adore and love her? Are there open lines of communication where both partners feel seen, valued and understood? Is there a deep emotional connection and mutual support?

5. Assess how they treat each other

Do they reject or dismiss each other's needs and perspectives? Do they approach their relationship with empathy, compassion and a willingness to compromise? Are they able to navigate conflicts and challenges as a team, finding solutions that benefit both of them?

6. Visualise the dynamics of their union

Are they operating in a traditional, hierarchical manner with one person taking the lead while the other follows? Are they actively collaborating, supporting and empowering each other as equal partners on the journey of life?

Exploring these questions will deepen your understanding of the balance between your feminine and masculine energies and shed light on the dynamics within your relationship. It is through introspection and honest reflection that you can cultivate a more fulfilling and harmonious connection within yourself. In this principle, you will have the opportunity to explore and answer these thought-provoking questions and gain a deeper understanding of the relationship you have with yourself.

Your feminine nature holds deep desires and deserves to have those desires fulfilled. Likewise, your masculine nature deserves recognition and appreciation for all that he does and provides. It is through the harmony of these two aspects that a fulfilling relationship with yourself can be cultivated. The feminine, representing grace, creativity and compassion, thrives when she is protected and provided for by her masculine. However, this can only happen when you are attuned to both aspects within yourself and they work in alignment. It is important to understand that the relationship you have with yourself is intricately connected to the relationships you form with your significant other(s). The way you treat and perceive yourself is reflected in how you engage with your partner and vice versa. It is a mirror reflecting back the dynamics of your self-relationship. By exploring these concepts and reflecting on your own experiences, you can gain valuable insights into how your inner relationship influences your intimate connections. This awareness opens the door to creating more fulfilling and balanced relationships, both within yourself and with others.

Let's discover how the masculine and feminine energies impact our attraction in relationships.

Attraction flourishes when there's polarity.

The stronger the contrast between each person's energy, the more magnetic the connection. Sexual polarity equals physical chemistry—that spark you feel when encountering someone with energy opposite to yours. When I first met my husband, there was so much attraction because I was in my feminine energy and he was in his masculine.

And when polarity is restored, attraction ignites.

However, in our marriage, when I was goal oriented and creating my business, we would fight, not realising I was meeting masculine energy with more of the same. When I was leaning into my masculine side, I came off tough and aggressive, like, 'What can you do for me? Can you keep up?' This doesn't work. When one person is in one energy, the other has to meet them with the opposite. We naturally dominate with one energy at our core. However, we move into the state of the opposite energy when needed.

Therefore, to find balance in your relationship, you need to be aware when your partner is in one power/energy, and you must choose the contrasting one at that time to relate without chaos. If your partner leans towards a feminine energy, show them attention, reassurance and understanding. Avoid making them feel overlooked, unsafe, unheard or misunderstood. Think of feminine energy like water—free-flowing and unrestricted—and the masculine as the protective cup that supports it. If your partner is in their masculine energy, it's best you choose to be in your feminine energy in order to express admiration, appreciation and openness. Avoid criticism, control or shutting them down. Vulnerability and nurturing is key to supporting masculine energy, so offer freedom and love instead. It's this freedom that will draw you closer, because that's what the masculine craves. This authenticity fosters a deeper connection and allows polarity to naturally emerge. Become aware when your partner resides in their feminine energy and when they lean towards their masculine. Choose to adapt the opposite energy within yourself to keep the spark alive and feel connected. Don't be discouraged if it doesn't happen immediately—view it as a beautiful journey of growth and self-discovery. Trust me, it's worth it!

Let's delve into the fascinating dynamics between the masculine and feminine powers within you and how they manifest in your relationships further. The way your masculine energy treats your feminine energy often reflects how your partner fulfils your desires and needs. Similarly, how your feminine energy treats your masculine energy can provide insight into how your partner respects and appreciates you. It's important to recognise that this reflection doesn't encompass every aspect of your partner's behaviour, but focuses on how they relate to and affect you personally. Paying attention to the parts that trigger you, the negative dialogue or any sabotaging patterns your partner may exhibit can be enlightening. These aspects can act as powerful indicators of any misalignment within your own energies. By examining these dynamics within your relationships, you gain valuable feedback about the alignment of your inner masculine and feminine energies. This self-awareness opens up the opportunity for growth, healing and fostering healthier connections within yourself, your partner and every relationship in your life.

Let's explore how these reflections work and the dynamic between your feminine and masculine aspects within yourself. Consider your closest relationship, whether it's with a spouse or partner, or even a past intimate connection or best friend if you're single. Reflect on how you feel about them and the quality of your relationship. The way you feel about your partner mirrors the relationship you have with your own masculine and feminine energies within. And the way your partner treats you is the reflection on how your masculine treats his feminine or vice versa.

The level of respect my partner shows me mirrors the respect I hold for both facets of myself. Similarly, my appreciation for my masculine aligns with how much my partner values me. The care my partner gives reflects the nurturing nature of my feminine side towards my masculine aspect. Respecting yourself translates to being respected by your partner. Appreciating yourself extends to feeling appreciated by your partner. Nurturing yourself reflects feeling held and loved by your partner.

Basically, the relationship you have with yourself (between your own feminine and masculine) is consistently reflected back to you by your partner and others. You have chosen them energetically to display your balance within. How you feel about yourself will be created in your outward world, mostly through your intimate relationships, to highlight what areas need addressing to gain deeper love for self. Know that you create situations and relationships that help with your evolution and to help you identify the love and worth you feel towards yourself.

Meeting your own needs sets the stage for your partner to meet yours. If you're not receiving what you need from your partner, it's likely because your own masculine isn't adequately supporting your feminine. If you feel rejected, mistreated or unheard by your partner, it could be a reflection of your own masculine energy mistreating your feminine. Similarly, if you don't appreciate or respect your partner, viewing them as weak or lazy, it may reflect how you perceive and treat your own masculine.

It's important to engage in meaningful conversations between your feminine and masculine side. It's essential to listen to your feminine, whilst also taking action in your masculine. It's crucial to love, respect and communicate with each other daily, working together to achieve your goals and live the life you truly desire.

Let's explore an example. A woman turns to her husband and expresses her desire to go to a luxury hotel for a weekend. Her husband responds, 'Luxury hotel? Sorry, sweetheart, but we can do a weekend camping.' In this situation, the woman feels triggered. It's important for her to look inward and address the issue within herself. The trigger serves as a reflection of something within her that needs healing. Resolving it starts with self-reflection between her two energies. It's important for both the masculine and feminine aspects within herself to come together and have a meaningful conversation intuitively. The feminine turns to her right side of her body (the masculine) and asks, 'Do you truly believe I don't deserve a luxury getaway?' The masculine turns to his left side (feminine side) and responds, 'I do think you deserve it, but I don't see how we can make it work.'

This is an example of how the masculine cannot attend to the feminine needs. He is feeling in lack and feels she is asking for too much, or that he isn't capable of achieving it. Therefore, the outward sabotage presents itself in the woman's life, through the lack of her husband who rejects her desire.

You see, the power to manifest our desires lies within us. If we believe we are unable to achieve something, how can we expect someone else to make it happen for us? In this example, the woman encounters an external reflection of her own inner misalignment.

The work to be done is internal. Instead of feeling that her partner or the outward world cannot provide for her, she needs to examine her own beliefs about why this desire seems unattainable. By nurturing the inner relationship and finding a healthy balance, she can create the life she truly desires. The most important relationship of all is the one we have with ourselves, as it sets the foundation for all other relationships in our lives, especially the intimate ones.

How we treat ourselves is reflected in our outward relationships.

Consider how your masculine energy treats your feminine energy. This is also a reflection of how others treat you. Similarly, how your feminine energy treats your masculine energy reflects how you treat others. These relationships serve as mirrors, showing you how you treat and love yourself. The measure of the love you have for yourself will determine how much you are open to receiving in this life. When you truly love yourself, you give yourself permission to pursue your dreams, to set healthy boundaries and to prioritise your own wellbeing.

You begin to attract positive experiences and people into your life because you radiate a sense of confidence and self-assuredness. But how do you cultivate self-love, you may ask? It starts with having a healthy relationship with your feminine and masculine energies. Recognise that *she* is worthy of love and deserving of everything she wants. Recognise that *he* is appreciated and capable of getting these desires for her.

Remember, you are not defined by your past mistakes or shortcomings, but rather by the infinite potential that lies within you. When you shift your mindset to one of self-love, you make space for growth and transformation. Self-love also means setting boundaries to protect your energy, prioritising yourself before others and giving yourself everything you desire. It also means being gentle with yourself and practicing self-compassion when things don't go as planned. Remember, self-love is not a one-off achievement, but a lifelong journey. It requires consistent practice and intentional effort. When you love yourself deeply, you become the best version of yourself, and you inspire others to do the same. Self-love is the foundation upon which a happy and fulfilling life is built. It's the practice of treating yourself with kindness, compassion and respect and knowing that you are worthy of love and happiness simply because you exist. It's understanding that you are the number one person in your life who you need to love, because when you do, everything else falls into place naturally.

> *You are only capable of loving others the exact amount that you love yourself.*

I had a client express to me the immense love for her children but admitted to a lack of self-love. I guided her to a transformative realisation—the depth of love for others is intricately tied to the love one harbours for oneself. I emphasised that her capacity to love her children mirrored her self-love. If she loves herself only marginally, that becomes the benchmark for the love she can extend to others. By expanding her self-love, she would unlock boundless potential for love, allowing her to cherish her children even more profoundly. This revelation illuminated the infinite possibilities that arise when one nurtures and expands their own capacity for love.

This formula is about learning to love and accept yourself fully, flaws and all. It's about embracing both parts of you and learning to use them to make a positive impact in your reality. It's about recognising your worth and knowing that you are deserving of love and abundance.

Often, we struggle to objectively assess our inner relationship. It is through our external relationships that we learn about ourselves and our inner state. Our closest relationships become our greatest teachers, surfacing areas in need of growth and healing. The people we attract into our lives are beautiful indicators of our internal balance. They reflect our desires and the lessons we need to learn. These reflections offer an opportunity to deepen our self-love and expand our belief in what is possible for us. When we value and honour these reflections, they create a shift in our internal balance, fostering personal growth and an increased capacity for love. Remember, we can only love another to the extent that we love ourselves. To build healthier and more balanced relationships, it's important to begin by loving ourselves. This self-love will then be reflected in how we engage with others.

Take a moment to reflect on your relationship with your feminine power.

- Are you honouring and cherishing her?
- Do you provide her with everything she needs?
- Are you listening to her?
- Is she creating ideas?
- Similarly, consider your relationship with your masculine energy.
- Are you loving and appreciating him?
- Do you express gratitude for all that he does for you?
- Is he capable, motivated and action driven?

By consciously nurturing both aspects of yourself and fostering a loving and appreciative connection, you lay the foundation for healthier and more fulfilling relationships with others.

Remember, the way we treat ourselves sets the tone for how others will treat us. So, let's prioritise self-love and create a positive ripple effect in our relationships.

EXERCISE
Explore your feelings between your feminine and masculine power

Let's delve into your feelings towards each other. Take a moment to reflect and write down your emotions. Consider how *she* feels about *him* and how *he* feels about *her*. Before you proceed, it's important to practise self-forgiveness and self-kindness. Recognise that you may not have been fully aware of the dynamics within your inner relationship. Be gentle with yourself as you uncover and reflect on how your dual sides treat one another. By acknowledging your past and current feelings, you open the door to greater awareness and understanding. This self-reflection will pave the way for a more conscious and fulfilling relationship moving forwards.

How Does She Feel About Him?	How Does He Feel About Her?
E.g. He is lazy He doesn't listen to her He ignores her	E.g. She wants too much She is impatient She is disrespectful

After doing this exercise, take a moment to reflect on how you feel about each other. Did you discover the intricate dance between your inner masculine and feminine energies? Are you in balance and harmony with yourself?

It's time to delve into the realm of emotions and uncover where the feminine yearns for understanding from the masculine and the masculine craves acknowledgment and appreciation from the feminine?

Imagine your feminine and masculine are always driving in a vehicle. The masculine is always the driver behind the wheel and the feminine is in the passenger seat, always directing. The feminine expresses where she wants to go (her desires) and the masculine, with attentiveness, navigates towards those aspirations to deliver (goal orientated) her every request. Yet, if imbalance arises, and the feminine is neglected or unheard, a cascade of negative emotions ensues, disrupting the harmony of this internal journey and she retreats to the backseat, disengaged. Likewise, it's the same for the masculine. If he feels like he can't obtain her desires, if he feels useless, or incapable, then he, too, retreats to the backseat. Both sides need to work in unison to understand, listen and achieve the desired results. Acknowledging these emotions becomes paramount for both sides to thrive. True harmony lies in the merging of their strengths, with the masculine steering and the feminine guiding, collectively reaching the desired destinations of a fulfilled and vibrant life, with both in the front seats of the vehicle. In this harmonious relationship within oneself, a healthy dynamic emerges when the feminine articulates her desires, the masculine responds with purposeful action. The ensuing gratitude and admiration create a sublime equilibrium.

Reflect upon this analogy and answer for yourself. Is your feminine directing, creating and loving? Or is she sitting in the back seat? Is your masculine, respecting, doing and supporting? Or is he sitting in the back seat?

Let's work out now how to get them in alignment with each other and unite as one in perfect balance and unity.

EXERCISE
Balance within your feminine and masculine

Let's engage in an activity that explores your feminine desires and how your masculine can fulfill them.

Column 1:
List all the desires your feminine has.

Column 2:
Why is he (the masculine) not providing this desire? (Consider the reasons why he may not be fulfilling her desires. Reflect on possible obstacles or limitations that prevent him from meeting her needs.)

Column 3:
How will he (the masculine) provide this desire? (Brainstorm ideas and solutions on how he can fulfill her (the feminine) desires. Think about potential steps he can take to make her dreams a reality.)
By examining her desires and the reasons behind her unfulfilled needs, you can help brainstorm ways for him to meet those desires. You can gain valuable insights into your inner relationship between your feminine and masculine power and find avenues for solutions, guiding growth, balance and unity within yourself.

List of Her Desires	Why Is He Not Providing This?	How Will He Provide This Desire?
E.g. To feel fit & healthy	Negative self talk, too lazy	Start exercising once a week. Eat 3 meals a day with 2 snacks and cut out sugar daily, (except 2 cheat days sugar is allowed)

Take responsibility and accountability for what you desire and start taking steps to fulfill those needs yourself. You have the ability, and deserve, to have everything you want, whether it's emotional, material or physical. Whether you're seeking more attention, love, affection, communication or even psychical things like a new car, holiday, job or relationship, know that you have the power within you to attain them. Embrace these incredible capabilities within yourself and work towards achieving all that you desire.

EXERCISE
Communicate with your feminine and masculine sides

To establish a harmonious balance within yourself, communication plays a vital role. Here's a simple daily practice for effective communication:

1. Start your day by connecting with your left side, representing your feminine

Ask yourself, 'What do you want today?' Listen attentively to her desires that arise within you.

2. Turn to your right side, symbolising your masculine and communicate your desires clearly

Ask for what you want and express your needs to your masculine. Request his attentiveness, understanding and cooperation in fulfilling these important desires.

3. Throughout the day, maintain open and honest communication between your feminine and masculine energies
Let him reassure her that he will honour and support these desires. This mutual understanding and agreement foster a sense of trust and partnership.

4. At the end of the day, take a moment to express your gratitude
Communicate your appreciation and respect for both your feminine and masculine sides. Express kind words that acknowledge their contributions and the balance they bring to your life.

By engaging in daily communication with compassion, appreciation and gratitude, you establish a healthy flow of dialogue between your inner energies. This paves the way for a balanced relationship within, where your desires are acknowledged and met, and harmony is nurtured within yourself.

Embrace your feminine and masculine power with love and respect, remember the greatest relationship you're looking for is already within you.

In the tapestry of my relationships, I recognise the threads of soul contracts, weaving lessons, growth and profound connections into the fabric of my life's journey.

PRINCIPLE 6

RELATIONSHIPS AND SOUL CONTRACTS

Welcome to the final principle, one that will resonate deeply with you because at our core, we're all beings of love. No matter what challenges we face, our fundamental desire is to give and receive love. This powerful principle of relationships and soul contracts helps conclude the weaving of *The Formula of Life*, encouraging you to go deeper into self-understanding and soar to rise higher. Each one of us has a unique purpose and specific lessons to learn, which contribute to the expansion of our consciousness. Within us lie inherent gifts and talents waiting to be discovered, nurtured and shared with the world. Often, it is through our challenges and difficult experiences that we uncover these hidden gifts.

Our relationships with others serve as powerful catalysts for self-discovery and self-realisation. It is through these connections, especially our significant relationships, that we encounter the necessary lessons and experiences that foster our growth. We can think of these relationships as prearranged contracts between souls, agreed upon before we entered this physical existence. These contracts serve as guiding forces, directing us towards the lessons and growth opportunities we need to fulfil our life's purpose.

According to certain mystical beliefs, it is said that we are accompanied by a group of souls throughout our different lives, ranging from three to twelve soul members. These souls form a cluster of energies that purposefully come together to create specific connections and relationships. Their presence is meant to facilitate our journey of self-discovery, growth and evolution. These souls travel with us from lifetime to lifetime, playing different roles to assist us with our life lessons and living our purpose. With each life lesson we encounter, we gain a deeper understanding of our true nature and unlock our capacity to expand in love, wisdom and personal power. These souls, known as our soul members in our soul family, play significant roles in our lives, taking on various primary relationships such as mother, father, siblings, intimate partner, in-laws and children. They are instrumental in helping us navigate our lessons and spiritual path so we can fulfill our soul's purpose.

In each lifetime, we take on different roles or characters that contribute to our personal growth and the evolution of others. The purpose behind this is to fully explore and experience the diverse aspects of our humanity and to directly engage with life itself. As we embody these roles, we have the opportunity to develop and evolve them, allowing each character to find their own unique meaning and purpose. Sometimes, while we are immersed in our earthly existence, we can become so deeply identified with our current character that we forget our ultimate goal of evolving and progressing. We may find ourselves stuck, unable to overcome the challenges presented to us, which hinders our ability to find true meaning and purpose in life. These challenges serve as valuable lessons and, if left unresolved, they carry over into future lifetimes. It's important to note that in the next lifetime, we may assume a different character or role, but we will continue to face the lesson we left unfinished in this life. Sometimes, life challenges become more intense and painful to help you recognise important lessons you might have missed before. If you're going through a tough time and have had a life filled with trauma, it could mean you haven't learned these lessons that have been trying to get your attention. So, they become louder, so you can hopefully hear them. Hopefully, with these stronger signals and after this principle, you'll finally understand and grasp the lessons meant for you.

Some of these soul agreements also involve karmic relationships. This means that in a past life, you might have done something to someone, and now they're returning the energy by doing the same to you. These karmic ties teach lessons and help balance out the relationship. It can be confusing when someone keeps hurting you in this life, but it might be because you hurt them similarly in a previous life. On a soul level, this is beneficial because it allows both souls to balance out the karmic relationship and move forwards by resolving the agreement made.

This emphasises the importance of learning and growing from your experiences, as they directly impact your soul's journey and your quest for personal evolution. It's crucial to grasp the lessons meant for you in this lifetime because in your next lifetime, you won't be consciously aware of your current soul's journey, however you will carry its wisdom. Neglecting these lessons will only magnify their impact in the next lifetime, so it is crucial not to overlook them. Why subject your soul to that? It's time to elevate and embrace all you're meant to learn, stepping into your purpose with clarity and determination, whilst you're here now.

Before we continue on our earthly journey, there is a spiritual process where contracts are established with each soul member that has chosen to come through with you. It's similar to creating a script for a play, where characters, scenes and events are carefully planned. The soul cluster, along with Source energy, engages in a council to review past challenges and growth.

For instance, let's say your soul seeks to learn lessons of self-worth, courage and independence. To facilitate this learning, various aspects are set up, choosing the characters and titles each soul member will represent, the story they will partake in with you and the overall environment. These elements are designed to both support and challenge you as the soul, creating relationships, interactions and narratives that fosters growth and development, all to help guide you to your life lessons and live out your mission.

Interestingly, for us to truly develop and grow, we are often presented with experiences that are the opposite of what we ideally desire. It's only when we experience contrast that we truly understand certain concepts. For instance, happiness is appreciated more after experiencing sadness, and courage becomes clear in the face of fear. These contrasting experiences play a vital role in our journey. Unfortunately, it's often pain and suffering that grab our attention and prompt us to reflect on the lessons we need to learn. When we find ourselves stuck in repeated patterns, it's a sign to pause and question what we're meant to understand. If learning were easy, we'd never delve deeper. We'd simply accept things at surface level.

It is through contrast that we obtain the lesson we need to learn.

The people who play significant roles in your life, even if they've caused you pain, are souls you've made spiritual contracts with. These souls deeply love you and have chosen to impact your life profoundly, even if it means taking on painful roles. You have negotiated and agreed upon these contracts before you arrived here. These souls want you to succeed and support your spiritual growth. For example, my father played a significant role in my life. We both agreed on a soul level that he would help teach me some of my valuable lessons I was here to learn, like self-worth, pride and confidence. This agreement we negotiated on a soul level involved him being abusive, narcissistic and manipulative, but we had confidence on a soul level, that I would learn and grow from these experiences to learn my life lessons and fulfill my purpose.

So, yes, it's true that the souls who have caused you the most pain actually hold the deepest unconditional love for you on a soul level. They willingly took on challenging roles to guide you towards your growth and evolution, despite the difficulties involved.

When we grasp this higher perspective and understand the purpose of our existence, we become better equipped to seek out the lessons and opportunities for personal growth. Instead of getting caught up in the roles and stories of our lives, we can shift our focus inward and connect with our true essence. It is within us that we discover acceptance, forgiveness, gratefulness and compassion. By viewing our life stories from this perspective, we begin to detach from the narrative and see things in a new light. We have the power to rewrite the script and explore new aspects of ourselves. In essence, we are finding new meaning, appreciating our life circumstances and uncovering our truth. This transformative process often involves dismantling our conditioned nature and reconstructing our lives in a way that aligns with our true essence.

I know it's a lot to digest, but here's the main point: the people who caused you the most pain in this lifetime are actually the ones who made contracts with you on a deeper level to help you learn and grow. I encourage you to forgive them and thank them from your soul, because on a higher level, you both agreed to these experiences for your growth and learning.

As we come into this world, the lessons begin early on in our childhood programming years. It's like we're set on a path right from the beginning, with no way to dodge what's coming our way. We begin learning our life lessons right from the get-go and often, those lessons start surfacing through our wounded child. But here's the twist. What we eventually realise is that the meaning the wounded child gave to the story, our lessons are actually its opposite. For example, 'I am not worthy' is actually 'I am worthy' (the lesson to be learnt). It's like the Universe has a wicked sense of humour, teaching us through unexpected twists and turns from the beginning.

As we all go through this *Formula of Life*, it is imperative as human beings living on this Earth that we undergo this process. We come into this world as pure love and it's essential for our growth, that through our pain and traumas we come to recognise the lessons needed so we can return to love. The soul contracts we have formed with our relationships begin to surface slowly throughout our lives, connecting us to our trauma. As we connect with these soul members, we become consistently triggered, which serves as a sign of what needs healing so we can evolve further. What a fun game. Talk about a wild ride! Seriously, once you wrap your head around it, it's like watching a sitcom—you can't help but laugh at the absurdity of it all.

Our relationships are a great indication of the profound insights of our life lessons. They serve as mirrors that reflect back to us what we need to learn and where we have room to grow.

In our relationships, both reflections and lessons are essential for our growth.

A **reflection** is something that lies within us and is presented through another person. If negative it reveals the unhealed parts of ourselves that we may not always be aware of and need to address. These reflections can be triggering and cause emotional distress, prompting us to react to protect ourselves. When we find ourselves passing judgment on someone else's behaviour that triggers us, it is an opportunity for introspection, to look within and see where that same behaviour or trait is mirrored in our own lives.

For example, if you are triggered by your partner being 'lazy', it's important to ask yourself, 'Where am I lazy in my own life?' Sometimes, it requires deep introspection to uncover how this laziness is playing out in different aspects of our lives. Perhaps you have been procrastinating about completing a project and the lesson is to explore the underlying reasons for your hesitation in sharing your business idea. It could be that you feel inadequate or lack confidence in your abilities. Reflections provide us with valuable insights into how we perceive and treat ourselves. By doing this inner work, we can identify our own blocks and limitations, which may be difficult to see within ourselves. Especially when the ego is in control. Through the behaviour of others, these blocks are brought to our awareness, allowing us to acknowledge our own negative aspects and take responsibility for our growth. Remember, the triggers we experience also carry inherent lessons for us to learn and integrate into our journey of growth.

While reflections often trigger us, **lessons** invite us to question on the situations presented to us, fostering curiosity and detachment to gain the necessary perspectives.

For instance, imagine being in a relationship where your partner subjects you to psychological, emotional and financial abuse. Your autonomy is stripped away. You are constantly blamed for the other person's moods, and you are consistently belittled. In this scenario, you may not experience triggers as much as deep pain and fear resulting from the loss of your sense of self. To navigate this difficult situation, you may find yourself repressing your voice, walking on eggshells to maintain peace and living in constant fear. You might not see as many reflections in this relationship compared to the lessons that are evident. The lesson in this situation lies in valuing your own life force and summoning the courage to leave the abusive relationship. By doing so, you learn valuable lessons about self-worth, courage, personal sovereignty and self-love. This transformative process of breaking free from the abusive dynamic propels exponential growth, turning pain into personal power. An abusive relationship can be very isolating and complex, and it is vital to ask for help and support when planning an exit.

Lessons in relationships have the potential to be profound catalysts for our growth, enabling us to discover inner strengths, heal wounds and cultivate resilience. Through these lessons, we can reclaim our sense of self, assert healthy boundaries and embrace the love and respect we truly deserve.

Relationships are powerful avenues for personal growth. They offer profound opportunities to learn about ourselves and others, fostering self-awareness, teaching us the importance of boundaries and aligning us with matters of the heart. At the start of a relationship, we often carry idealised expectations, hoping for perfection. However, it is when disturbances and challenges arise within us during the relationship that true growth takes place. The dynamics experienced in our early childhood, particularly between our parental figures, greatly influence our later relationships. Unhealed aspects of our parents are projected onto us, shaping our conditioned behaviours. Moreover, generational trauma in our ancestral linage can be inherited and requires healing. If our ancestors and parents didn't address their inner struggles, we may find ourselves inheriting these patterns and needing to find the courage within ourselves to break the generational cycle. Someone in your family linage has to heal and break the pattern of these traumas. Might as well be you! You're already doing the work anyway.

In the grand dance of energies and universal laws, we attract specific partners throughout our lives who play crucial roles in our healing journey. Whether it's our current significant partner or the most recent intimate relationship, if we're single, they serve as catalysts, helping us untangle the intricate web of profound lessons and learnings we're meant to undergo in this lifetime. Interestingly, painful dynamics between ourselves and our parents are often mirrored in our intimate relationships.

This reflection serves as an opportunity to bring the unconscious aspects of these dynamics into conscious awareness. By recognising and addressing these patterns, we can work towards healing ourselves and transforming our relationships. By delving into the depths of our relationship dynamics with our *parents*, exploring the influences from our *childhood programming years* and acknowledging the *generational patterns at play*, we embark on a journey of personal growth and the potential for breaking free from destructive cycles. Through self-reflection, compassion and a commitment to healing, we can create healthier, more fulfilling relationships that align with our true selves. Our ancestral trauma, our parent's unhealed aspects and our wounded child are the three indicators to discovering of list of lessons we have for this lifetime.

EXERCISE
How your relationships determine what you need to heal

Let's look at your relationship with your parents so you can further determine what you need to heal. Write five words that best *represent* each parent. (List both the light and dark aspects.) You can do more than 5 if you want but keep the number consistent to all.

MUM	DAD
1.	1.
2.	2.
3.	3.
4.	4.
5.	5.

Now write five words that best *represent* your partner. (List both the light and dark aspects.) If you are single, list the most significant relationship you have had in your life. If you've never had an intimate relationship, there will be a friend of significance.

PARTNER
1.
2.
3.
4.
5.

1. Circle all the negative aspects from Mum, Dad and Partner and then rewrite them below.

_____

_____

_____

_____

_____

_____

_____

_____

_____

_____

2. Next to each negative aspect, ask yourself, 'Which aspect is found in me, which aspect is found in my partner and which aspect is in both of us?'

3. Place your initials, or your partner's, or both, next to each negative aspect.

4. Now flip each negative aspect to the opposite. (The negative aspects present in your parents, your partner and yourself serve as catalysts for understanding the **lessons** you are here to learn.)

E.g.	Weak	Strong
	Rude	Kind
	Negative	Positive

5. Now list the opposite positive word and place the words 'I am' in front of each. (Feel free to add the light aspects here as well.)

E.g.   I am Strong
        I am Kind
        I am Positive

_____

_____

_____

_____

_____

_____

_____

_____

_____

_____

Welcome to your life lessons!!!

6. Turn these into your daily mantras. Repeat them throughout the day, especially when faced with situations that usually trigger negative feelings. Replace those moments with these positive affirmations like 'I am powerful'. Remember, you've spent a lifetime absorbing negative influences from your parents' wounds, childhood programming and ancestral trauma. Now is the time to take control and nurture what needs to be healed within you.

When you start healing on this level, it sends positive ripples throughout your reality. Your subconscious isn't fixated on negative evidence from past trauma anymore. Instead, by focusing on positive aspects, you'll start noticing evidence of the progress you're making. But remember, it takes effort. Repeat these affirmations daily for at least thirty days to start with and keep doing so whenever you feel vulnerable.

Keep in mind that when you shift your subconscious beliefs from limiting to limitless, your external world begins to transform. This impacts how you engage in your relationships as you gain a deeper understanding of the new, empowered version of yourself.

You might wonder, *'What about my partner? Do they change, too?'* The answer is yes and no. They may not actively be doing the same inner work as you, but because you're no longer reacting or being triggered by past wounds, it can shift the dynamic between you. When your mind isn't fixated on negative evidence, everything can change for the better.

As you heal and transform your subconscious beliefs, you'll start seeing evidence of your new mindset, gaining more control over your world. Your reactions begin to alter, and you respond differently to your parents, your partner and those closest to you. This will change your perspective and appreciate them on a deeper level for the lessons they've taught you. In your mind, you understand the lesson and in your heart and soul you cultivate gratitude for the teachings. You can now let go of the pain they have caused you, because it was in your own suffering that you actually needed to learn from. This awareness helps you rise higher and guides you to align with your life's purpose.

This exercise is also designed to assist you in recognising and comprehending the unresolved elements within your family lineage that have persisted across generations. Now is the moment for you to step forward, raise your hand and take on the responsibility of healing these patterns, not only for yourself but also for your children or future descendants, thereby affecting your entire ancestral DNA lineage.

As you've realised, the relationships that have given you the most pain, the most hurt, are the strongest souls that, on a soul level, love you the most. These are the souls that you have negotiated with to learn your biggest lessons and they have put up their hand to play a certain role to help guide you towards learning these lessons.

With this expansive understanding, *place your hands on your heart* and send them forgiveness alongside gratitude. Thank them on a soul level for all they have taught you and are still teaching you. They do not know the roles they're playing, but you do. *You're the conscious one, comprehending both yourself and them.* Remember, you're also playing a significant role in their lives as part of their soul group, teaching them lessons in return. We're all participants in the same cosmic game. Armed with this knowledge, you can elevate your play and navigate with greater wisdom and compassion. Your soul members play specific roles to facilitate these lessons, and it's essential to thank and love them unconditionally, even if it is only energetically. Remember, each member, including yourself, has agreed to these roles for collective growth and empowerment, enabling you to embrace your highest potential and reconnect with the love at your core. If you have disassociated yourself with any one of your soul members in your life, be conscious of the lessons they have taught you. Learn it and elevate. You can close a contract once you have learnt and returned to peace and love within yourself and towards that soul. Absolutely it's fine not to be in contact with them, especially if they cross your boundaries. However, the work needs to be done within your own being so the contract is understood, and all lessons have been learnt, otherwise another soul will walk into your life to finish off the work. In other words, you can't escape the lessons you are here to learn. Only when you have learnt, you can be at peace with that relationship on a soul level and appreciate the role they have chosen to play for you. Just know that we are all responsible and accountable for our own lessons.

Through discovering some of your lessons, you can now gain insights into where patterns have occurred and what really needs to be healed. If you have recurring patterns, they are attached to lessons that are needing your attention. Reflect on what you might need to heal within yourself. Are you noticing any patterns or repeating cycles in your relationships that your parents represent? This awareness can provide valuable insights into the lessons you're here to learn.

Now, consider how you are progressing with these lessons. Are you actively learning and growing from these experiences? Take some time to reflect on your personal journey and the steps you are taking to heal and overcome any challenges. By understanding the aspects that require healing, and being aware of the lessons presented to you, you can commit to a transformative journey of self-discovery and personal growth. Remember, healing is a process and by consciously working through these aspects, you can create healthier and more fulfilling relationships in your life.

For instance, when we notice negative patterns, we can focus on moving forwards towards more positive outcomes. It's important to understand that we can't avoid or bypass the lessons we've contracted upon for our personal growth and evolution. Relationships, even if they are not ideal, serve as catalysts for our growth. They often reflect the parts of ourselves that we felt were missing in our earlier years. When others can't fulfil those needs, we may project our anger, disillusionment and pain onto them. Relying on others to fill our gaps or provide the safety and security we long for can create co-dependency and hinder our personal development.

We must recognise that it is impossible for someone else to fulfil what can only be fulfilled within ourselves. Expecting others to meet all our needs will ultimately lead to disappointment in varying degrees. Blaming and projecting onto others only prevents us from healing and growing. When we engage in the necessary inner work, it transforms our relationships and attracts healthier dynamics. As we grow internally, we begin to mirror that growth in the relationships we attract. By focusing on our own healing and personal development, we open ourselves up to more enriching, well-balanced and fulfilling connections with others.

Be grateful for your lessons as they have made you who you are today.

So proud of you!

WHAT NOW?

Now it is time to celebrate the abundance of wisdom you have absorbed, because knowledge is the ultimate power. The greater your understanding, particularly of yourself, the greater you will triumph, conqueror and achieve your visions. This moment marks not the conclusion, but the beginning of a profound journey into self-discovery. Now you have complete insight into the depths of your being, understanding the workings of your mind and the intricate depths of your soul, grasping your lessons and honouring your soul contracts. Now, with purpose as your guide, you shall navigate life consciously, expanding the horizons of your existence.

Now, life flows effortlessly by choosing peace, joy and love for yourself. This transformative journey towards self-love commences now with immense intensity. Hold yourself accountable and commit to consistency in your efforts. Commit to revisiting this book and all its contents as often as necessary, whenever the urge strikes to maintain the momentum of your reprogramming and to honour all the work you've accomplished so far.

This formula serves as your compass on your journey to true power. You will find solace in revisiting its pages, a ritual that ensures you are consistently reshaping your subconscious beliefs into clear manifestations of your desired path. Cultivate consciousness in your thoughts and emotions, recognising the daily progress made in diminishing the influence of limiting beliefs. Empower yourself with this new knowledge that you now possess. Be proud that you can now catch your negative thoughts as they arise and promptly flip them and assert control over them and your feelings. With this new-found clarity, watch as your visions effortlessly materialise into reality.

However, I need you to know that within the depths of your subconscious are layers of beliefs awaiting to resurface. Just when you believe you've conquered them and learnt their lessons, a new challenge emerges to test your resolve and true embodiment. Embrace the realisation that your subconscious mind has lots of power, consistently influencing and overriding your conscious thoughts. You need to be more aware of them than ever and now that you know what they are thinking, you have the power to flip them and consciously choose the opposite. When you think you've learnt a lesson, the Universe often tests you to ensure you've truly grasped it. During these tests, your awareness needs to be sharp. Remind yourself, *'This is just a test from the Universe, but I've got this. I'll stay true to my new beliefs.'* Through daily diligence in addressing these beliefs, you gain mastery over your mind. With each triumph, you diminish their influence, ultimately shaping the life you envision. You've got this.

This book is your personal treasure, a sacred manuscript just like a cherished journal. It is yours forever, not to be passed around. However, consider recommending it to the significant individuals in your life because surrounding yourself with conscious people can greatly enrich your own journey and, of course, theirs as well.

You've become your own healer, equipped with valuable insights from this transformative formula. You can now share these gifts with your children, your partner, your parents, your schools, your communities and beyond. In embracing consciousness, you unlock the profound ability to comprehend your true essence and the mechanics of our creative power. My intention is not only for your amazingness to shine through, but to unite in this journey of self-discovery and empowerment with those that surround you. You can now enrich lives and illuminate the path to collective awakening. Imagine a world where each individual can embrace accountability, self-love, deep self-awareness and empowerment and have the tools to heal themselves. Such a vision holds the promise of a profoundly improved existence for all.

However, for now, your awareness of self will act like a ripple-effect, extending beyond yourself and will be felt by those closest to you, particularly within your own home. Initially, the transition may seem challenging to some, even to yourself. You need to acknowledge how your vibration has heightened, and you need to navigate through the turbulent waters because you will notice the change in your relationships and the world around you. It's now time to become patient because you know more. Give others time to adjust to the evolving dynamics. As you embody your highest self, your responses naturally shift, prompting others to adapt to your transformation. Through your example, may you inspire those in your tribe to embark on their own transformative paths, fostering a collective journey towards greater fulfilment and authenticity.

Now, you grasp the concept of energy and recognise that you're not just flesh and bone. You are a spiritual being experiencing life in a human body. With this understanding, you realise that the world is brimming with endless opportunities waiting for you to explore, all available at your fingertips.

Now, you realise that you're not just in the universe, but a vital part of it. You possess incredible power beyond what you've ever imagined. You are connected to Source and Source is connected to you. By discovering your purpose and syncing with the right energy, you are aligning yourself for success. It's clear: the Universe is on your side because it lives inside you.

Now, you have the depths of self-awareness, understanding your subconscious belief system and making the decision to regain control from the power of the wounded child. Now it's time to nurture your inner wounded child and begin the process of healing the trauma by reprogramming your childhood wounding. Remember, the wounded child is attached to the ego and once you see the ego, it automatically goes away. It's time to quieten the chaotic chatter of your mind and purposefully select your thoughts. In this silence, you become very aware when the wounded child is speaking. You can feel it like heat in your body. Catch it, nurture it and tell it that you no longer give it power. The victim is gone. Now you begin to reprogram your limiting self-beliefs and, with this newfound mastery, you begin to create your desired reality, continuously ensuring that your vision remains under your control. No longer does your subconscious thoughts dictate your reality. Instead, you have control over them. You are now the master of your thoughts and feelings, firmly in control of your own destiny. You are the driver, and the subconscious is in the boot of your car, where you no longer listen to it.

You now have the innate ability to harness the power of positive thinking, create alignment, comprehend the intricate dance of vibrations and understand the law of attraction. Recognise yourself as a magnetic force within the universe, continuously drawing back into your reality that which you project outward. Take accountability for the creation of your life, acknowledging that any misalignment with your desires stems from your thoughts and emotions. Through deliberate shifts in your mindset and feelings, you pave the way for the manifestation of your desired reality. Remember, you are the architect of your own existence, sculpting your reality with every thought and emotion you cultivate.

Now, you have the amazing revelation of the intricate balance between your light and dark sides of your being. Through unconditional love for both, you transcend duality, embodying wholeness. Know that each facet serves your highest good. Embracing both grants you a powerful understanding of your truth, freeing you from the need for apology or justification. You have realised the light does not always serve you, just as the dark sometimes does. Both aspects enrich your existence in ways, empowering you to navigate life's varied landscapes with authenticity and grace making you whole.

Now, it is time to embark on the journey of radical self-love, embracing and balancing both your feminine and masculine power into harmonious unity. This marks an infinite and breathtaking love affair—the most captivating love story you'll ever experience; the one with yourself. Recognise that this relationship with yourself reigns supreme above all others, serving as the reflection to your outward relationships. The reflections that are mirrored back to you by others, especially your intimate relationships, serve as messengers, illuminating areas of growth and self-sabotage. Know that internal triggers are an indication of where you still need communication and support between your own masculine and feminine power. When inner unity is achieved, you harness the boundless power to love yourself unconditionally, overflowing with love to share generously with others. Within you lies the inherent ability to love yourself completely and unconditionally.

Now, you grasp the profound concept of your relationships and soul contracts—agreements made between each soul, meticulously crafted to guide you through life's lessons and revelations. With this newfound awareness, you perceive your loved ones through a fresh lens, recognising their unwavering support in your journey towards realising your fullest potential. It's time to extend forgiveness, gratitude and understanding, acknowledging the roles each soul has played in your life, and vice versa. You've come to understand the ancestral lineage of trauma passed down through your generations and now you boldly raise your hand to take responsibility for healing these deep-seated wounds within your DNA's ancestral tapestry.

By now, you've likely grasped the truth that your journey is yours alone to navigate, with responsibility and accountability resting solely on your shoulders. While connections with others enrich our lives, the depths of our innermost feelings remain an enigmatic treasure, known only to ourselves. This inherent gift, this sacred secret, lies at the core of your individuality—a testament to the deeply personal nature of self-discovery. Embrace the realisation that your emotional landscape is yours to explore and cultivate, for you alone hold the power to shape your reality. It's time to bid farewell to the victim within, for that tired narrative no longer serves you.

With newfound clarity and unwavering resolve, step boldly into a future defined by emotional intelligence and profound self-love. Welcome to your healing journey—a continuing path of growth and enlightenment, where each day presents an opportunity to elevate your spirit, rise your vibration and expand your consciousness. Be committed, remain ever accountable, ever responsible, ever consistent. Witness with awe as the Universe conspires in your favour, unveiling miracles before your very eyes. The seed of transformation has been planted. Now, with tender care and relentless determination, nurture its growth. By engaging in this formula, you've been activated with light codes that will awaken awareness and consciousness within you. Be gentle with yourself as you uncover and release old patterns that no longer serve your highest good. Now is the time for change, for transformation, for the magnificent rebirth of your truest self.

All eight billion humans of this Earth go through *The Formula of Life*, yet you stand as the fortunate one, armed with the tools and techniques to delve deep into its mysteries and unravel its logic. Now, empowered by this understanding, you possess the clarity to discern your past creations and chart a new course for transformation. With a wealth of knowledge at your fingertips, you can navigate the intricacies of human existence and the depths of your spiritual essence with profound insight and wisdom. You have recognised the extraordinary gift of your existence. Before we arrive to this Earth, apparently, we yearn to partake and experience the very pain that appears alluring from afar. But once we are here, all we want to do is escape from it. Through my own journey, I've come to understand that embracing pain and darkness is essential, for therein lies the gateway to the light. It becomes our sacred duty to transmute pain into power, for it is through our darkest moments that we gain profound insights into the nature of light. Our pain and trauma, once viewed as a burden, now flows as the fuel of our healing journey. I've come to realise our pain is the most exquisite gift, the catalyst for our extraordinary self-love and understanding. Today, I speak of my trials with a smile, for I recognise them as sacred contracts, meticulously negotiated for my soul's growth. Every experience, every hardship, has sculpted me into the healer, the guide, the empowered individual I am today. Embrace, appreciate, respect, be grateful and forgive your pain, for in doing so, you reclaim your power and step boldly into your truth. This, my friend, is my wish for you.

The Formula of Life is a beacon of empowerment, guiding you on a journey of self-discovery that transcends the veil of amnesia. As you awaken to your true essence, you radiate consciousness not only to yourself but also to those around you and the world at large. Through dedicated practice of these six principles, you unlock the boundless reservoir of gifts within you, ascend to higher vibrational realms and become part of the *New Earth*. The 'New Earth' is a world of existence characterised by higher consciousness, harmony, peace and spiritual evolution. It's envisioned as a shift away from the current state of humanity, marked by conflict, suffering and environmental degradation, towards a new era of unity, compassion and ecological balance. This idea is associated with spiritual teachings, esoteric beliefs and metaphysical concepts, suggesting a transformational shift in human consciousness and society as a whole. I now welcome you to this new reality.

In the company of friends and family, your new heightened awareness will allow you to discern truths hidden between the lines without the need for preaching. Your role is simply to remain rooted in your own journey of growth, for ultimately, each individual must grant themselves permission to embark on their own healing journey. While you can offer guidance and recommend the path, the transformative work must be undertaken by each individual themselves. It is a personal journey of self-reclamation and empowerment, one that only they can navigate.

The journey of self-discovery is a gateway to understanding the intricacies of the world around you. Through embracing *The Formula of Life* and immersing yourself in its six principles, you undergo a metamorphosis that illuminates every aspect of your life and being.

Now you are equipped with powerful insights, you have gained a heightened ability to discern the behaviours, thoughts and emotions of others. You'll effortlessly identify victim mentalities and negative narratives, recognising their impact on your own vibration. As you ascend to higher realms of consciousness, your tolerance for negativity has had a transformative shift. Stay in your power and don't let others dim your light. Trust in this process, for within this elevated state, you attract like-minded souls, high-vibrational opportunities and alignment with your true self. In this sacred space of alignment, you'll find yourself surrounded by the energy and resonance you've always yearned for.

Let me share with you the awe-inspiring truth: embarking on this journey is the pinnacle of self-discovery, an exhilarating adventure filled with joy, illumination and empowerment. Each day, as you deliberately choose your thoughts and feelings, nurturing your relationships and honouring your soul contracts, you'll witness the miraculous unfold before your eyes. With crystal-clear vision, unwavering precision and alignment in your emotions, you'll effortlessly manifest your deepest desires. Now the Universe conspires in your favour, showering you with blessings beyond measure.

You've arrived, dear friend, and I am bursting with pride at your accomplishment.

Now, go forth and embrace the extraordinary life that awaits you.

It is done. It is done. It is done. Empowered by the magic of three, it is done.

And so it is.

DEAR PARENTS AND FUTURE PARENTS

I want to begin by saying that you are all incredible. The fact that you have taken the time to undergo this formula and are seeking to better yourself is truly a testament to the dedication and love you have for yourself and your family. As parents, our greatest responsibility is to raise the most conscious children possible. I truly believe that it is through this conscious parenting that we can make a real change in the world.

The future belongs to the most conscious generation, and it all starts with you. By healing your own wounds, stepping into your power and living in your truth, you are setting the foundation for your children to do the same. With *The Formula of Life* in your hands, you now have the tools and techniques to help your children through their programming years and even guide them to reprogram their own stories. Remember, children are like little sponges and the way they are raised in their environment has a great impact on their overall balance. Healing yourself as a parent is a critical component in raising conscious and healthy children. When you heal your own wounds, you break the cycle of negative traits, trauma and programming that have been passed down from generation to generation. By doing this, you set your children up for success, providing them with a foundation that is free from the limitations of the past.

The knowledge and tools presented in this book will allow you to recognise and catch your negative beliefs, giving you the power to guide your children to do the same. As you heal yourself and become more conscious, you will be better equipped to support your children when they face their own challenges. Through your example, your children will learn the importance of self-awareness, resilience and self-love. You will be able to catch their negative impacts and redirect them towards positive beliefs, guiding them towards a life of positivity, possibility and fulfilment. As you continue on your journey of healing and growth, you will be creating a more conscious world, one where parents are empowered to raise the next generation of conscious and healthy children. Remember, the work you do on yourself today will impact generations to come. Embrace the tools and techniques in this book and together, let's create a brighter future for our children and our world.

Healing trauma is crucial for parents because unresolved emotional wounds can be passed down through the generations. Parents who have experienced trauma, whether it's from their childhood, previous relationships or life experiences, may unintentionally project their unhealed emotions and behaviours onto their children. When children are exposed to unresolved trauma, they may develop negative coping mechanisms, patterns of behaviour and belief systems that hinder their growth and happiness. This can lead to a cycle of trauma and suffering that is perpetuated from one generation to the next. By addressing and healing your own trauma as parents, you can break the cycle and prevent your children from inheriting your emotional wounds. This not only benefits the children, but also creates a healthier and more fulfilling family dynamic. Parents who have healed from their own trauma are better equipped to support their children's emotional needs, and they can create a safe and nurturing environment that promotes growth and development. In short, healing your own trauma as a parent is a powerful way to break the cycle of generational trauma and create a brighter future for your children.

As a parent or an aspiring parent, you hold a tremendous responsibility to shape the lives of your children. The way you raise your children has a direct impact on their emotional, mental and physical wellbeing. Therefore, it is ideal that you take the time to heal yourself before bringing kids into this world or while raising them. If you already have children and are just beginning this work, don't be discouraged—it is still deeply worthwhile, both for them and yourself. As you grow and improve, your children follow suit. They're an extension of you, embodying the healing and growth within your family. Healing yourself from past traumas, limiting beliefs and negative patterns is crucial, as it ensures that you don't pass them down to your children. When you do the inner work and heal your wounds, you automatically break the cycle of negative ancestral lineage that has been passed down from one generation to another. This allows your children to start their lives with a clean slate, free from the burden of negative programming.

The journey of healing yourself can be challenging, but it is undoubtedly worth it. When you are in a state of healing and growth, you set a positive example for your children to follow. Children learn by watching their parents and when they see you prioritise your wellbeing and do the inner work, they learn the importance of self-love and self-care. They learn to take responsibility for their own emotional health and wellbeing and they become more resilient in the face of challenges. So, if you are a parent or a future parent, I urge you to be open to change and vulnerability. Take the time to do the work, because by doing so, you will help your kids rise. Remember, you cannot give what you don't have. You cannot pour from an empty cup. Therefore, it is essential to dump your emotional baggage before you dump it on your children. By doing the work, you eliminate the pressure of your trauma towards them and create a healthier and happier home environment.

I encourage you to be great so that your kids can be great, too. By healing yourself, you create a ripple effect of positive change that can impact future generations. Your children deserve the best version of you and the only way to achieve that is by doing the inner work. Remember, it's never too late to start. Begin your journey of healing today and watch as your life and the lives of your children transform in beautiful ways. Create a household that inspires growth, accountability, responsibility and conscious awareness of self. Guide your children in ways that reflect their uniqueness, foster their passions and encourage curiosity. And most importantly, have fun along the way! Remind your children that failing is a part of success and that their affirmations and positive mindset can set them up for a successful future. Teach them to explore the unknown with excitement, to embrace their lessons and to get back up when life knocks them down. The healing journey is a beautiful and continuous evolution that we must all commit to as long as we are alive. It's important to keep going, keep reading, keep learning and keep meditating. Whatever helps you along your path, do it! You possess the power to heal yourself, and you can empower your children by teaching them that they have that same ability within them.

Remember, the pain and trauma may never fully go away, as they have many layers, but through having a deeper understanding of yourself and healing, it becomes smaller and more manageable. The triggers become less intense, and peace becomes more familiar. When you notice yourself feeling calm instead of triggered or at peace instead of angry, you'll see just how far you've come. And then, one day soon, you'll realise the deep sense of peace within you and no matter what circumstance presents itself in your outward world, nothing can disturb that peace. This journey is about rising into your power and being the best version of yourself. By just finishing this book, you've taken an important step. Now it's up to you to keep doing the work. Keep releasing and letting go of the trauma and pain. Revisit the exercises when you feel you've gone off track. Write new lists every so often. Keep evolving, growing and shining your light. You're doing great and the world needs you to keep going. You are here for a reason and now it's time to shine your light, step into your power and rise higher.

My greatest wish is that we awaken as a whole. Imagine a world where we are all accountable, understanding, self-aware and consciously connected with compassion and love. Imagine a world of peace, wouldn't that be amazing? However, some things we have no control over, but one thing is certain, we have control over ourselves, our thoughts, our feelings and choosing joy and peace within. By living in alignment, purposefully and consciously, you inspire others to do the same. This frequency affects those around you, making a difference in your own life and in turn, making a difference to others. You have the power to spread positivity for all, throughout your family, your community and beyond.

So, dear parents and future parents, *go deeper, rise higher*! Embrace this journey of self-discovery and transformation and watch as you and your family flourish to the best version of themselves.

With love,
Rena xx

ABOUT THE AUTHOR

Rena Harvey stands as a distinguished figure in the realm of healing. She is a teacher, healer, mentor, and fellow traveller on the profound journey of self-discovery and exploration. Her dedication to empowering others and her unyielding pursuit of knowledge have shaped her into a beacon of hope and transformation in the lives of those she touches.

Rena's journey commenced with a Bachelor of Education in Secondary School Teaching coupled with a Bachelor of Arts, sparking her lifelong love of learning and marking her early career as an educator.

Her profound love for all things spiritual, a deep calling within her soul and an unwavering sense of purpose in this world, led her to dedicate herself to healing. Consequently, she embarked on a journey to acquire extensive knowledge and hone her skills, ultimately attaining the status of Usui Reiki master practitioner and qualified sound therapist. These accomplishments, intertwined with her shamanic practices and holistic counselling expertise, have empowered countless individuals to transcend their pain and embrace their inner power. Rena's mission is clear: to empower individuals to unlock their fullest potential, discover their authentic selves and step into their ultimate power. Clients who have been fortunate to work with Rena can attest to her warm and compassionate approach. Her vast knowledge and unwavering guidance serve as beacons of clarity in their journey towards self-discovery and healing from years of complex, deep-seated trauma. Rena is a practitioner who genuinely embodies the principles she imparts, drawing on her extensive personal experiences and the transformative journey she has undertaken. After dedicating thirty years to her personal spiritual healing journey, Rena adeptly assembled the myriad pieces of wisdom acquired from spiritual mentors, gurus, masters and teachers. Bringing together this insightful accumulation of knowledge, she created *The Formula of Life*.

She possesses a deep passion for travelling the world and exploring diverse cultures, immersing herself in their unique ways of life, beliefs and communities. In addition to her professional pursuits, Rena skilfully balances the demands of raising a family of three children, with the unwavering love and support of her husband.

Rena is available for either in-person sessions or online consultations and also hosts powerful, empowering speaking engagements, courses and retreats on *The Formula of Life*.

🌐 renaharvey.com.au 📷 @renasharvey ✉ hello@renaharvey.com.au

www.ingramcontent.com/pod-product-compliance
Lightning Source LLC
Chambersburg PA
CBHW030548080526
44585CB00012B/308